ILLUSTRATOR'S REFERENCE MANUAL

NUDES

ILLUSTRATOR'S
REFERENCE
MANUAL
NUDES

CHARTWELL
BOOKS, INC.

A QUARTO BOOK

Published by Chartwell Books
A Division of Book Sales, Inc.
110 Enterprise Avenue
Secaucus, New Jersey 07094

ISBN 1-55521-507-6

Reprinted 1992

The book was designed and produced by
Quarto Publishing plc
The Old Brewery, 6 Blundell Street
London N7 9BH

Photographer: Peter Hince
Assistant: Roberto Bortali
Designers: Penny Dawes, George Ajayi
Editor: Sally MacEachern
Art directors: Nick Buzzard, Moira Clinch
Editorial director: Jeremy Harwood

Manufactured in Hong Kong by Regent Publishing Serices
Limited
Printed by Lee Fung Asco Printers Limited

Contents

Using the nudes manual

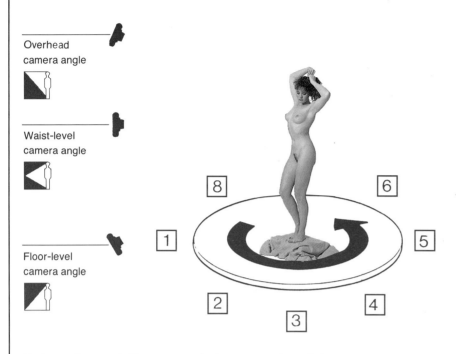

Overhead
camera angle

Waist-level
camera angle

Floor-level
camera angle

8			6
1			5
2			4
	3		

The ILLUSTRATOR'S REFERENCE MANUAL:
NUDES comprises 56 poses categorized under seven
general headings. Each category has a code number,
and within each category each pose has a further
subcode number for ease of reference. Male and
female nudes are each divided into three basic
categories: standard poses, classic poses based on
works of art, and glamour poses. The final category
consists of couples in classic poses. Within each
category the poses are grouped into lying, sitting and
kneeling, and standing.

Each pose is presented from 24 angles. The images
are as large as the pose will conveniently allow.
Consequently, although a consistent scale is
maintained within the camera angles on each page,
the scale changes from one page to another within
the same pose. In order to facilitate the drawing of
group illustrations, a simple calibrated bar
accompanies each set of camera angles which are to
the same scale. To draw a pose combining two or
more figures, use a visualizing camera to enlarge or
reduce the calibrated bar on chosen angles until a
precise match is obtained. This will ensure that the
figures are all drawn to the same scale.

Each pose is presented from
24 angles,
achieved by using three
cameras, and a turntable
rotated through 360° (above). A

simple camera angle symbol
(above left) accompanies the
relevant group of images within
a pose.

Waist-level camera angle

Floor-level camera angle

FEMALE GLAMOUR - SITTING

5.06 Temptress

FEMALE GLAMOUR - SITTING

Temptress 5.06

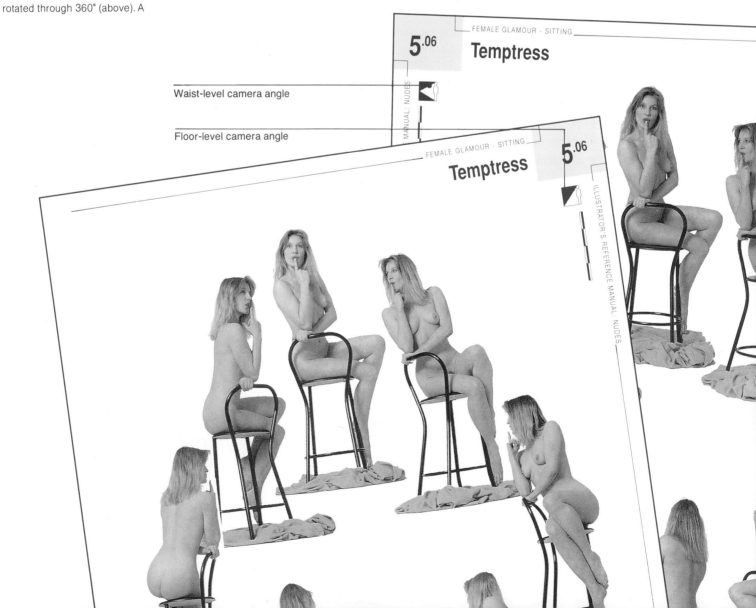

Group illustrations (left) can easily be drawn. The calibrated bar accompanying each pose can be used to standardize the scales.

Pose title   Category heading

Code number

FEMALE GLAMOUR · SITTING

Temptress   **5**.06   Subcode number

Overhead camera angle

ILLUSTRATOR'S REFERENCE MANUAL · NUDES

Calibrated bar

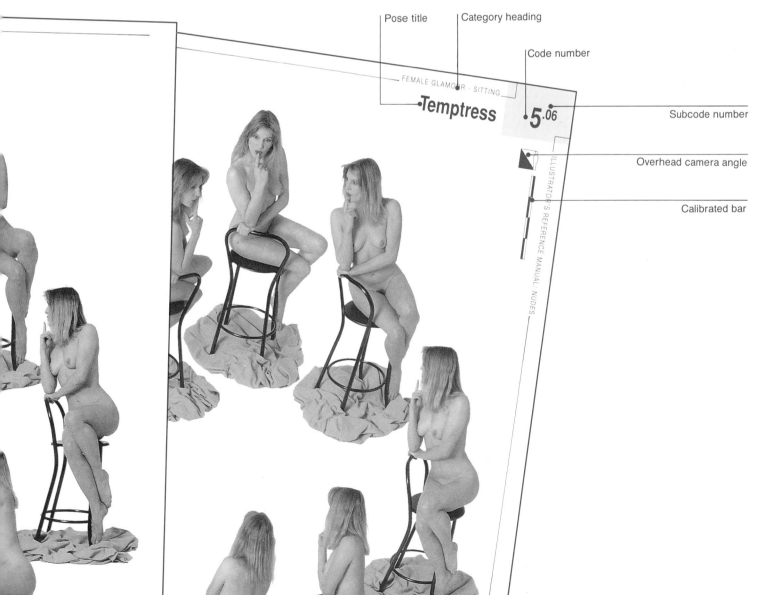

1.01

Sleeping beauty

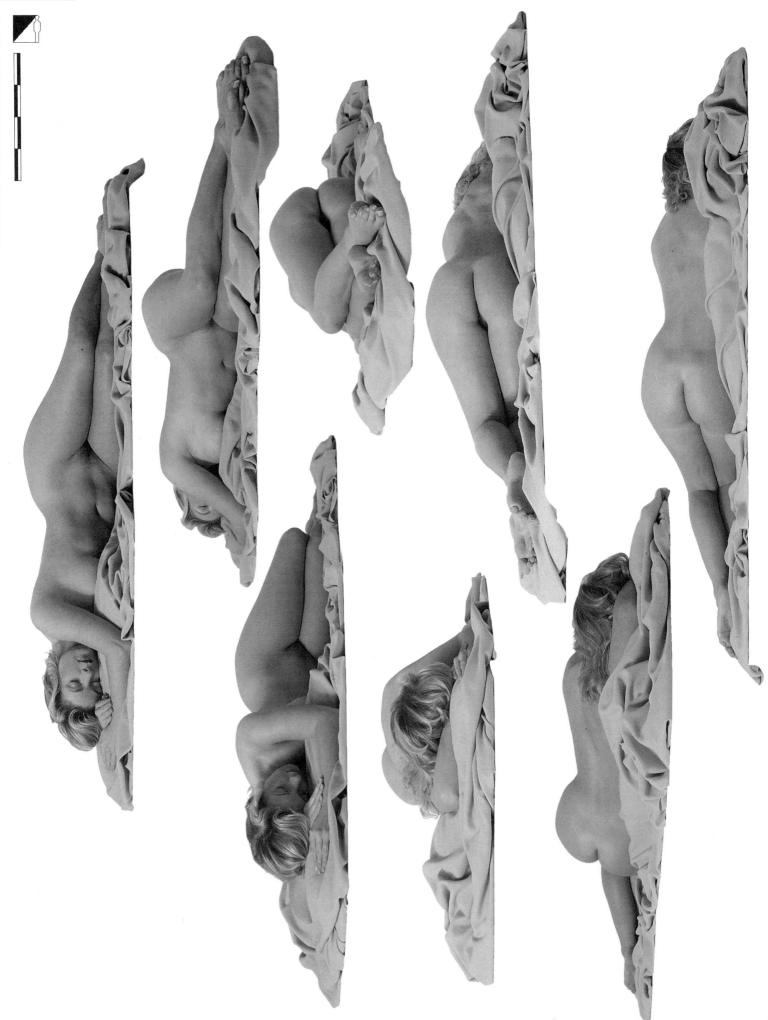

Sleeping beauty

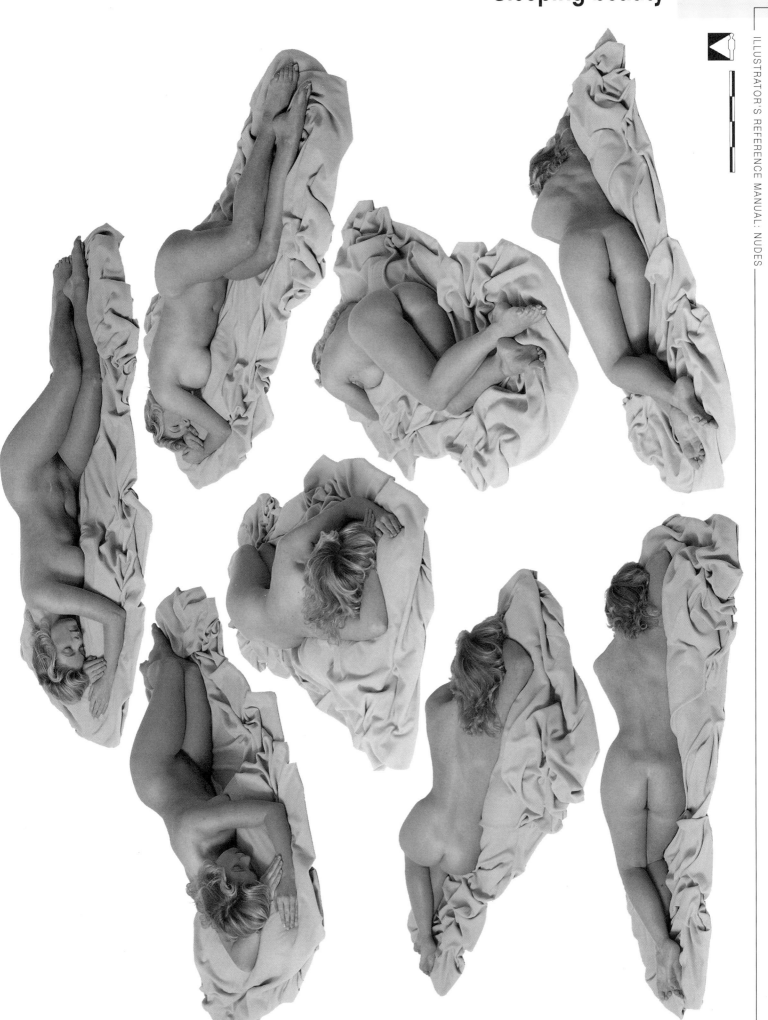

Sleeping beauty

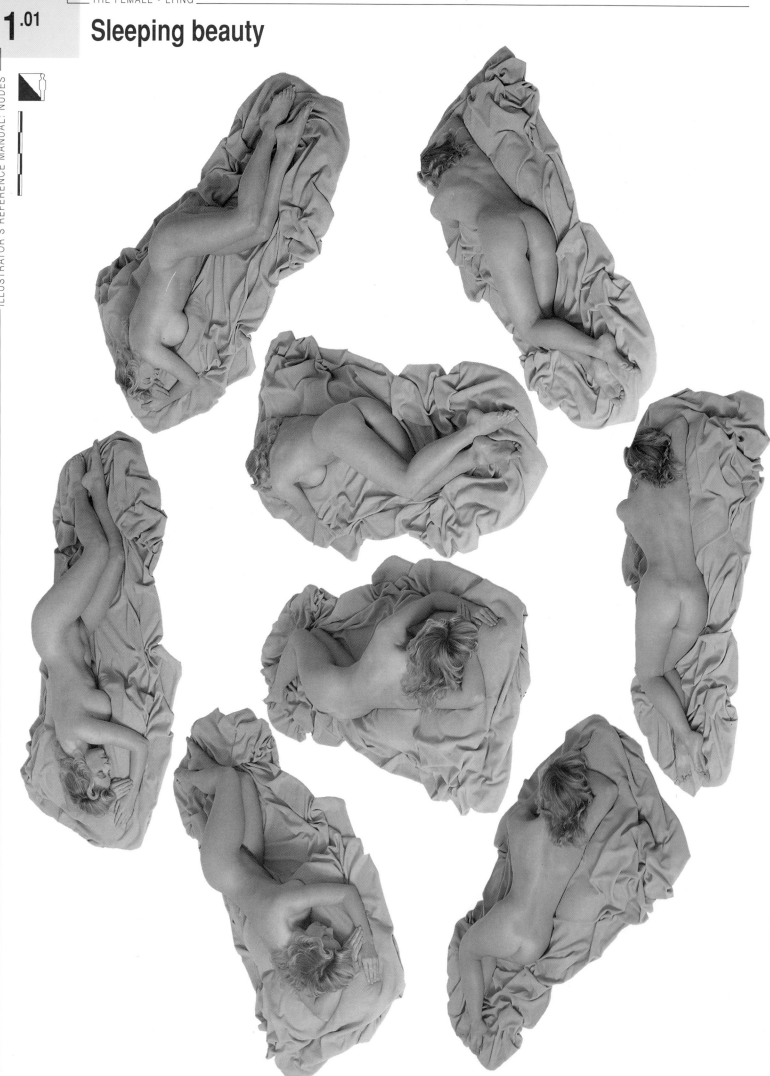

Contemplation

Contemplation

Contemplation

Winsome ways

Winsome ways

1.03

Winsome ways

Hand on hip 1.04

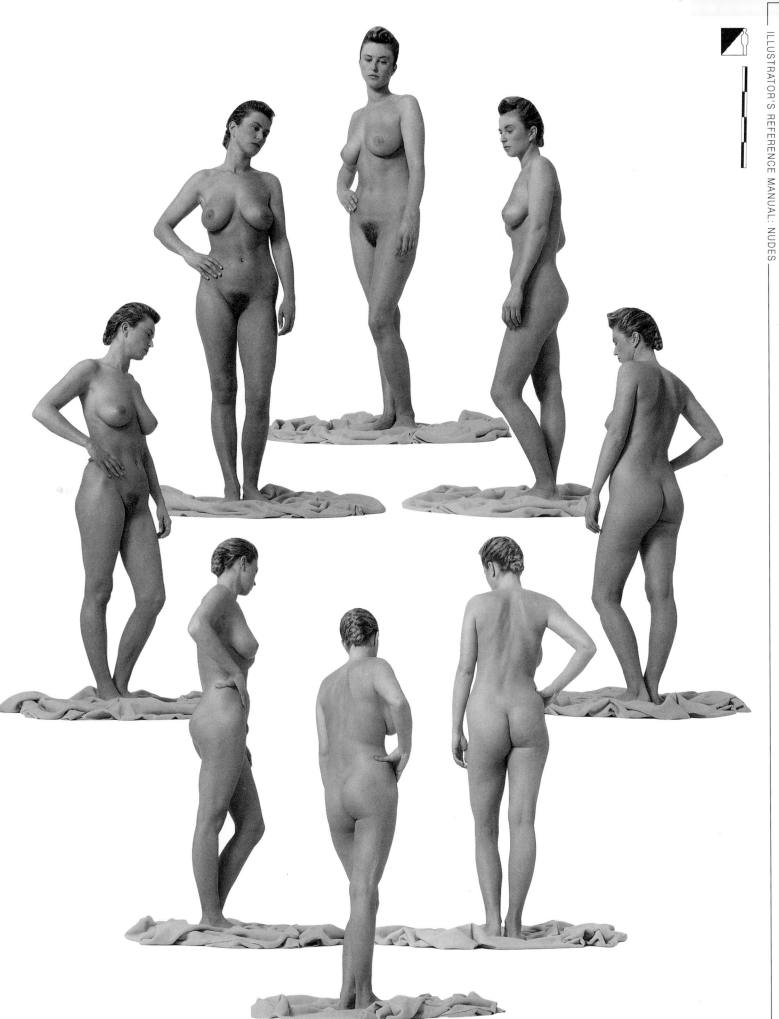

Hand on hip

Hand on hip

Striding forth

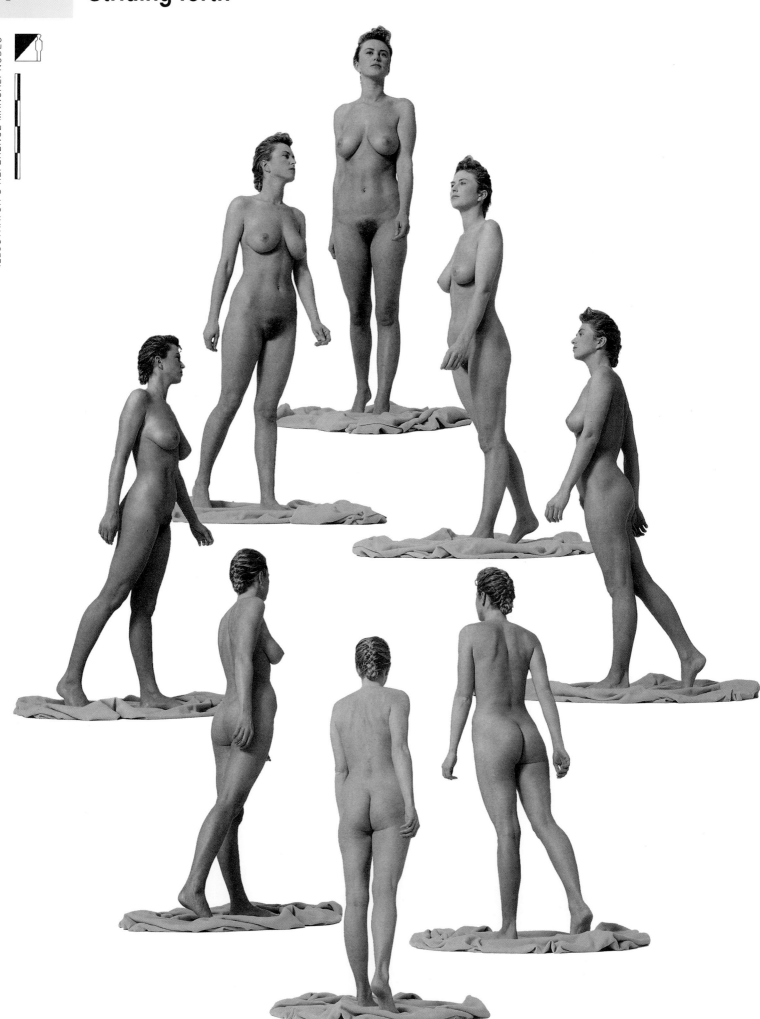

Striding forth

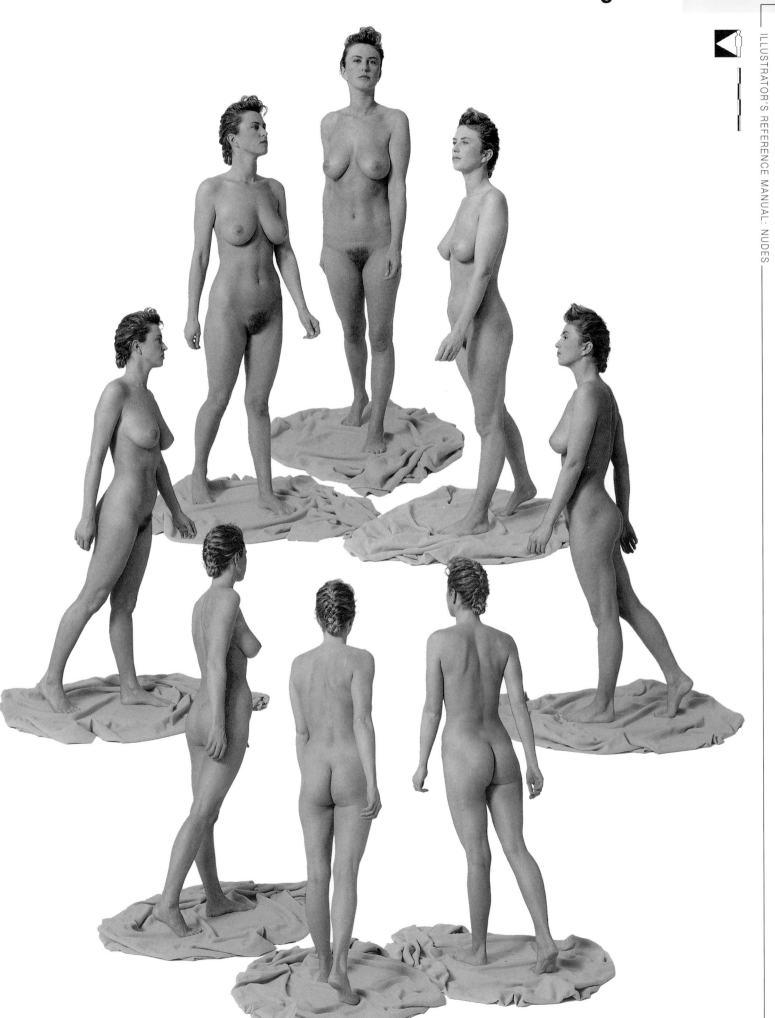

1.05

Striding forth

Exhaustion

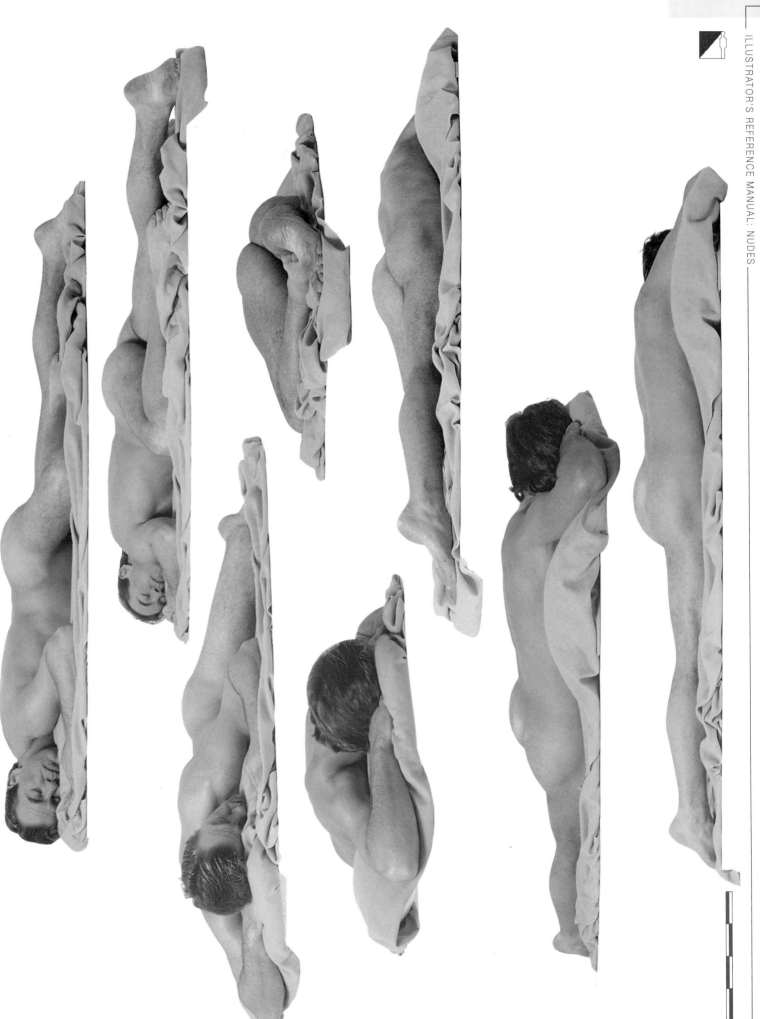

2.01 Exhaustion

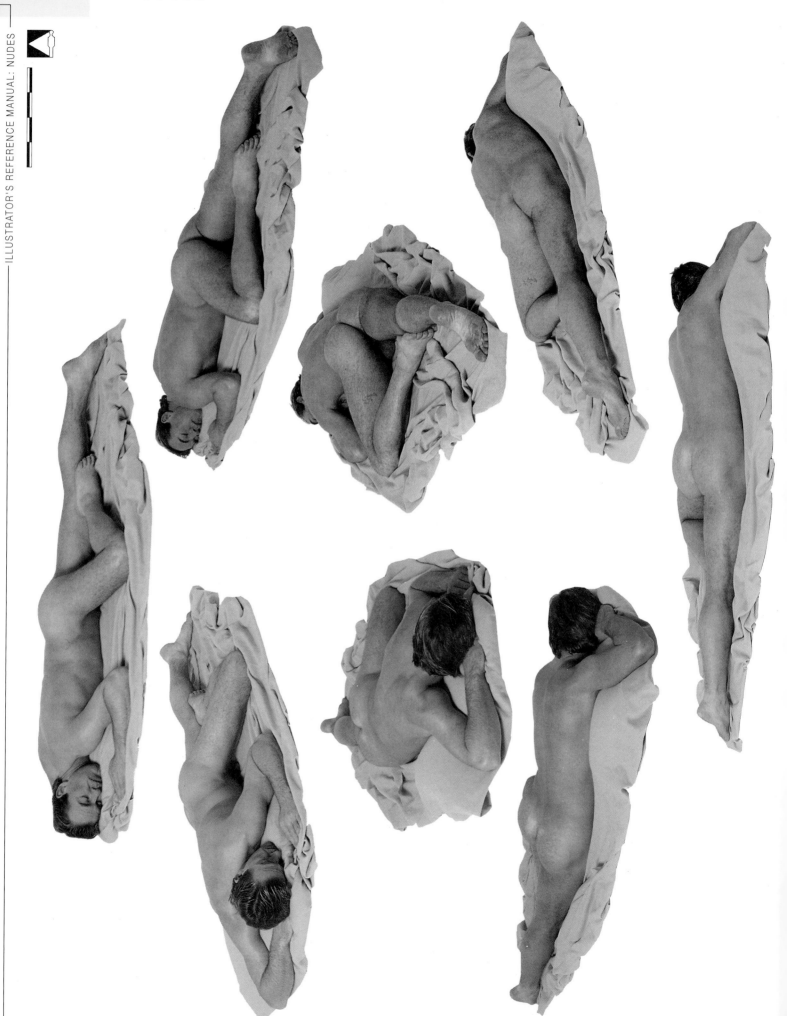

Exhaustion

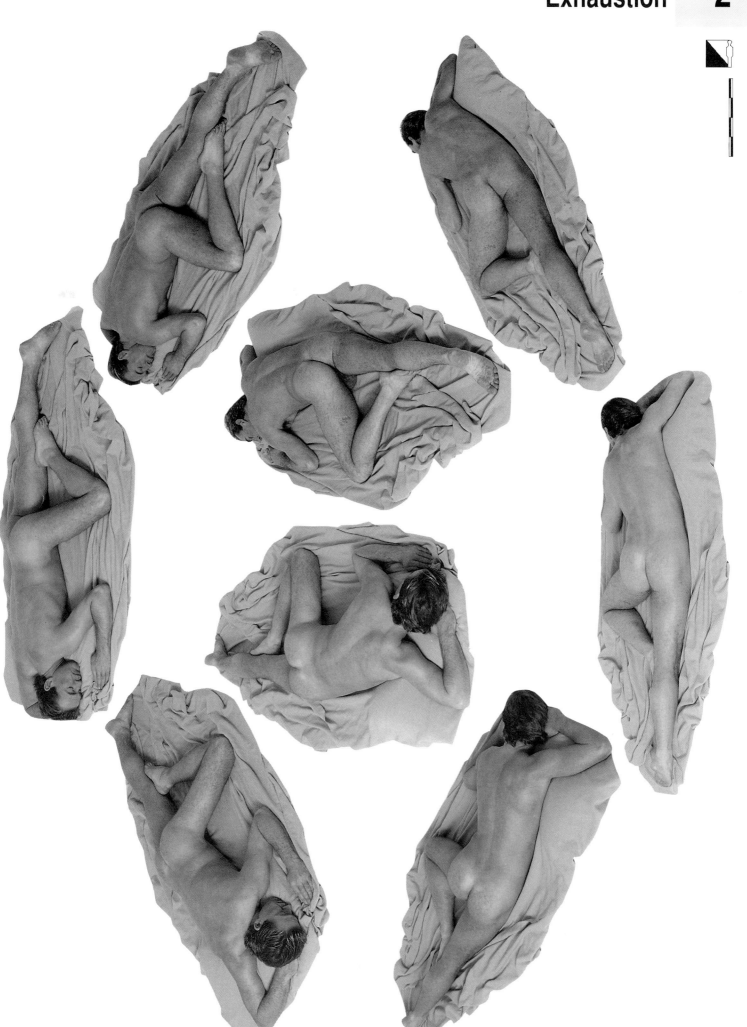

Introspection

Introspection

Introspection

Arms folded

2.03

Arms folded

Arms folded

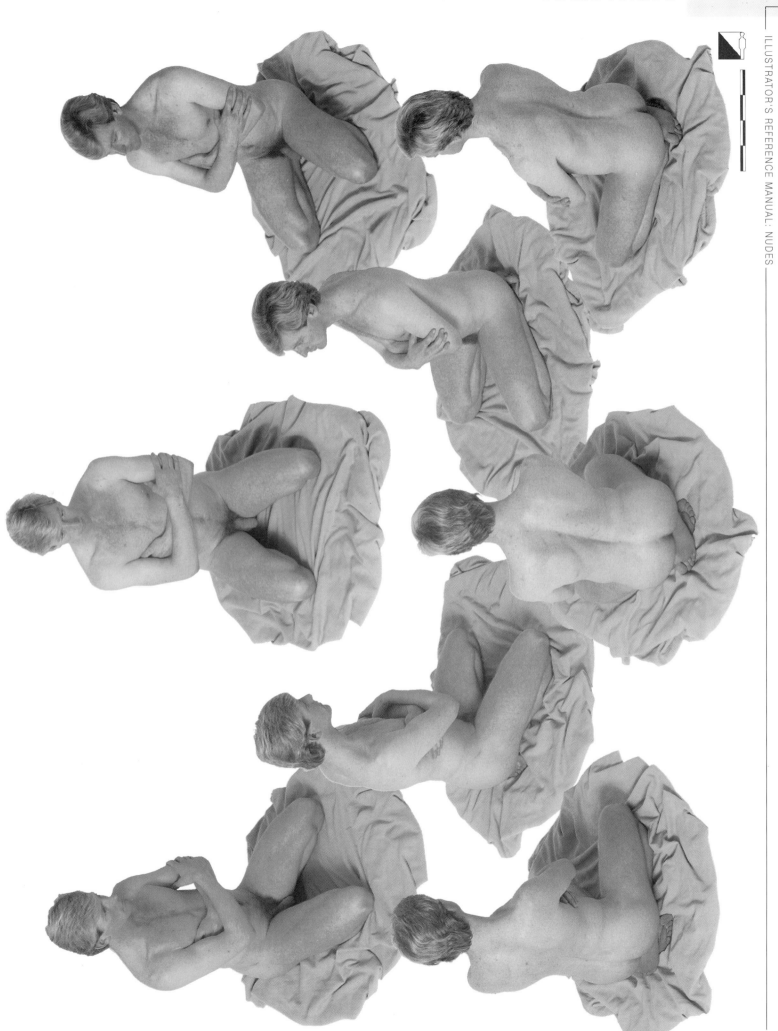

Arms crossed

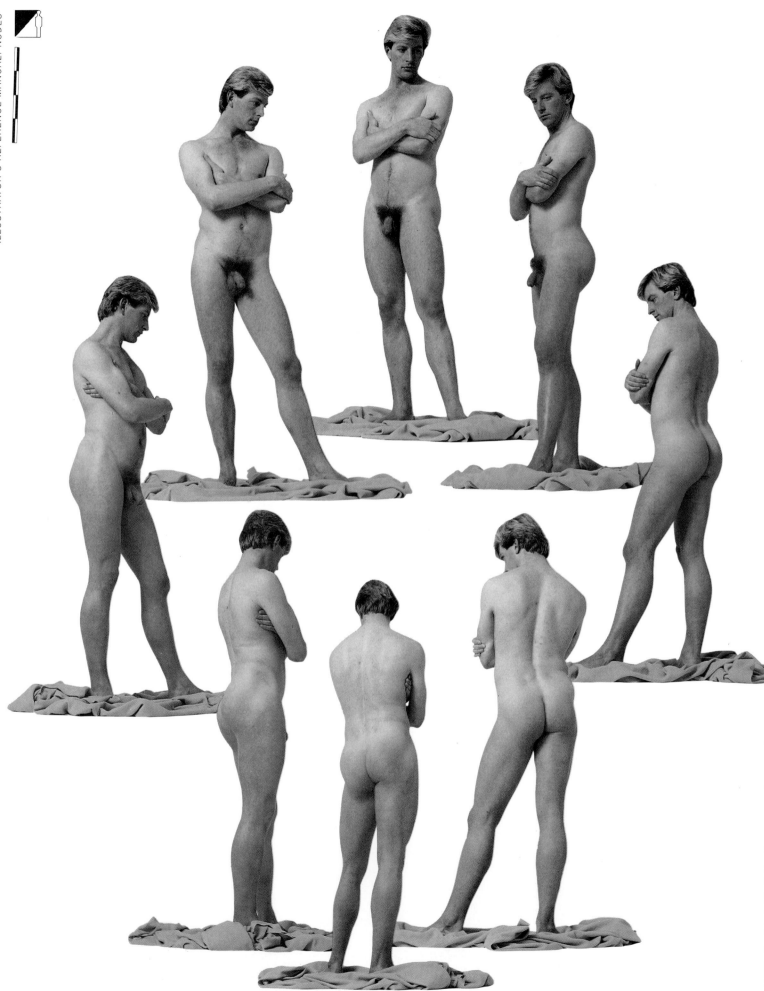

2.04

Arms crossed

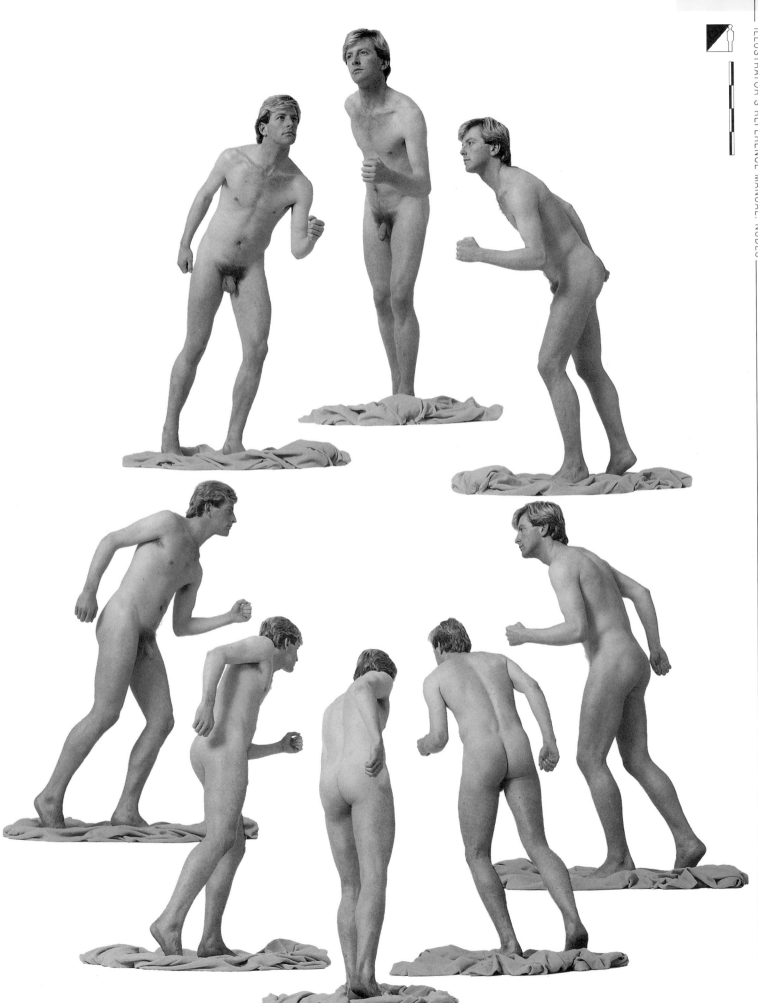

Sprinting

Venus

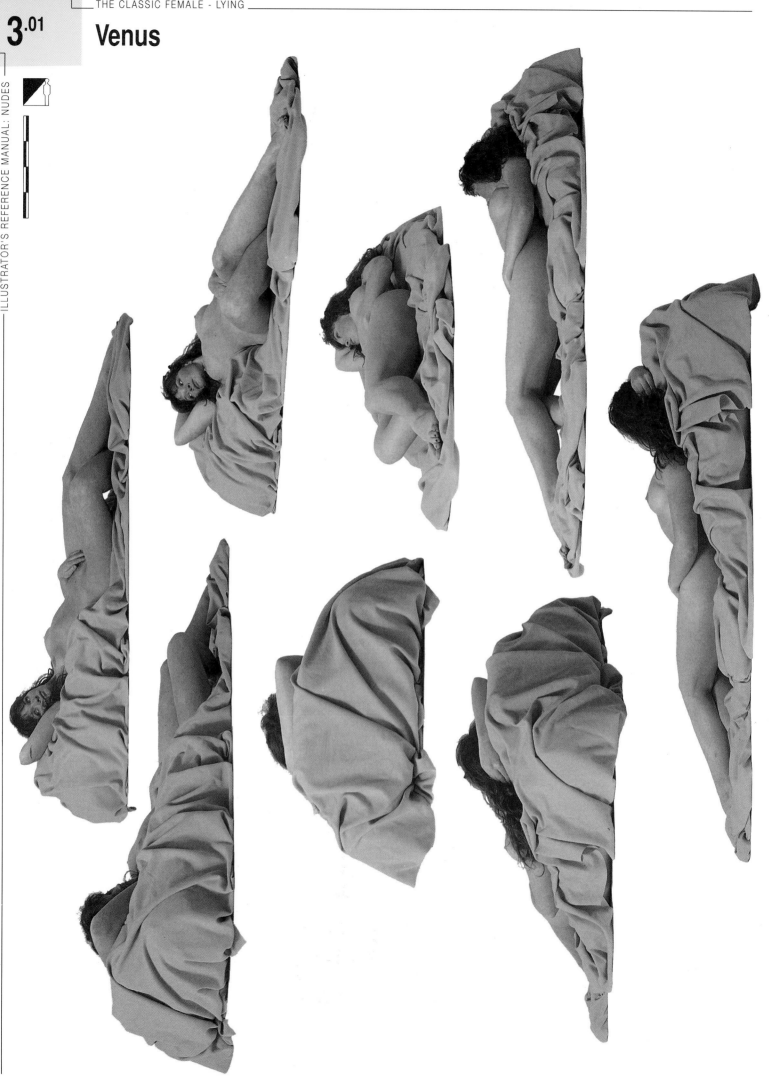

Venus

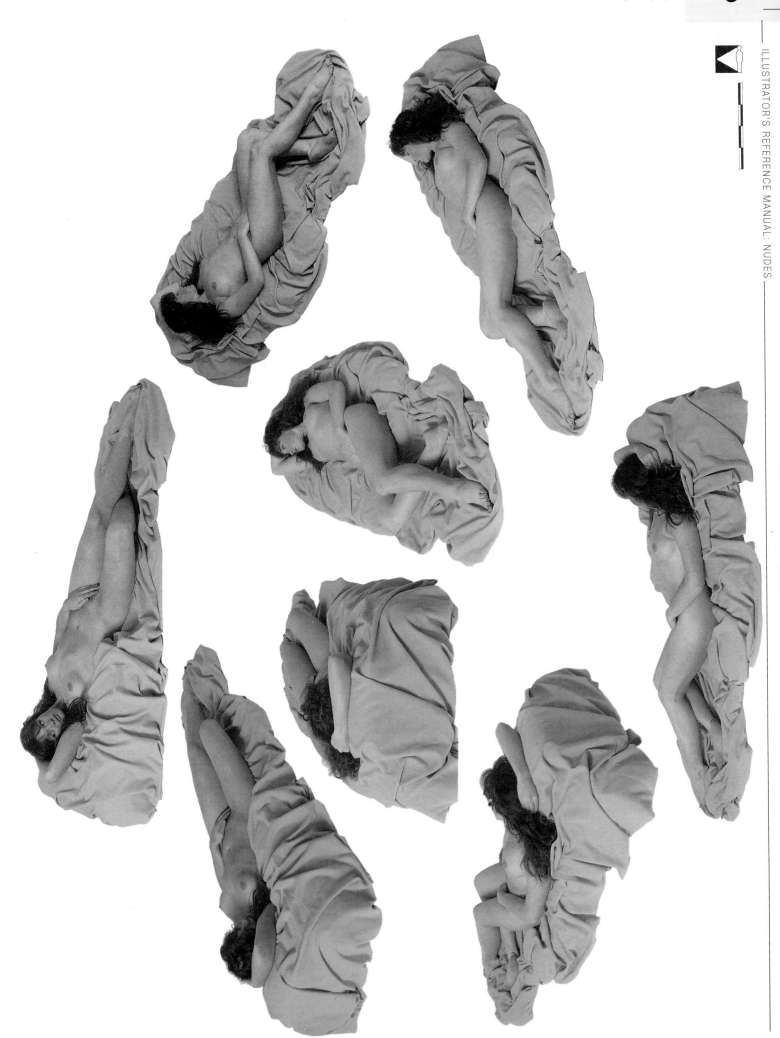

3.01

Venus

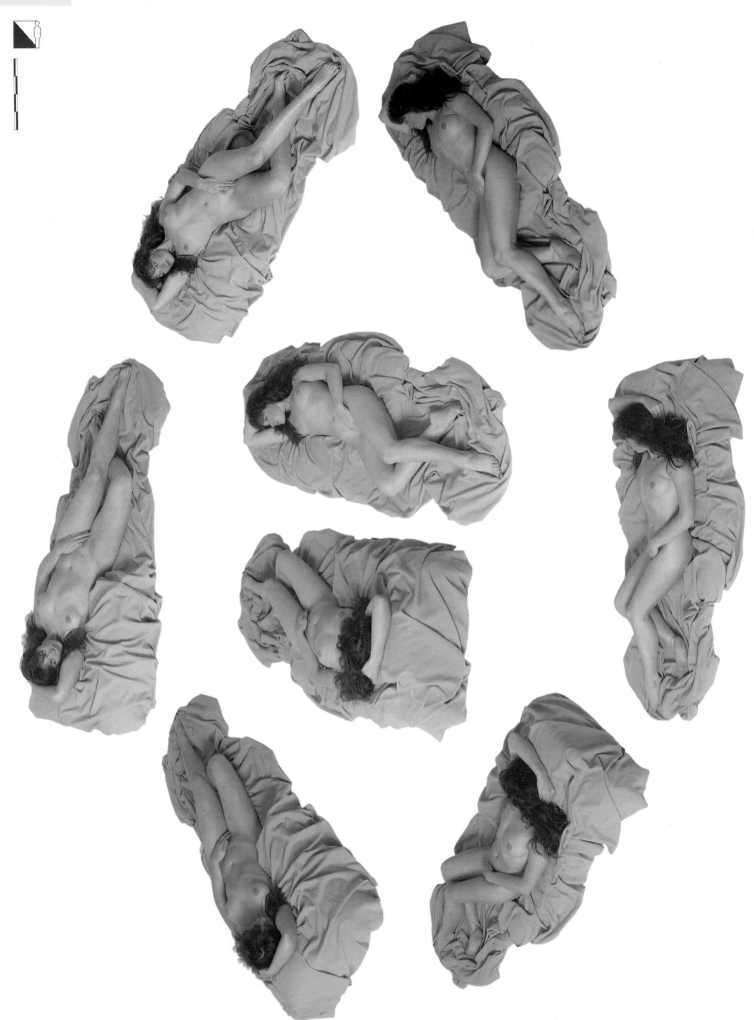

The mistress

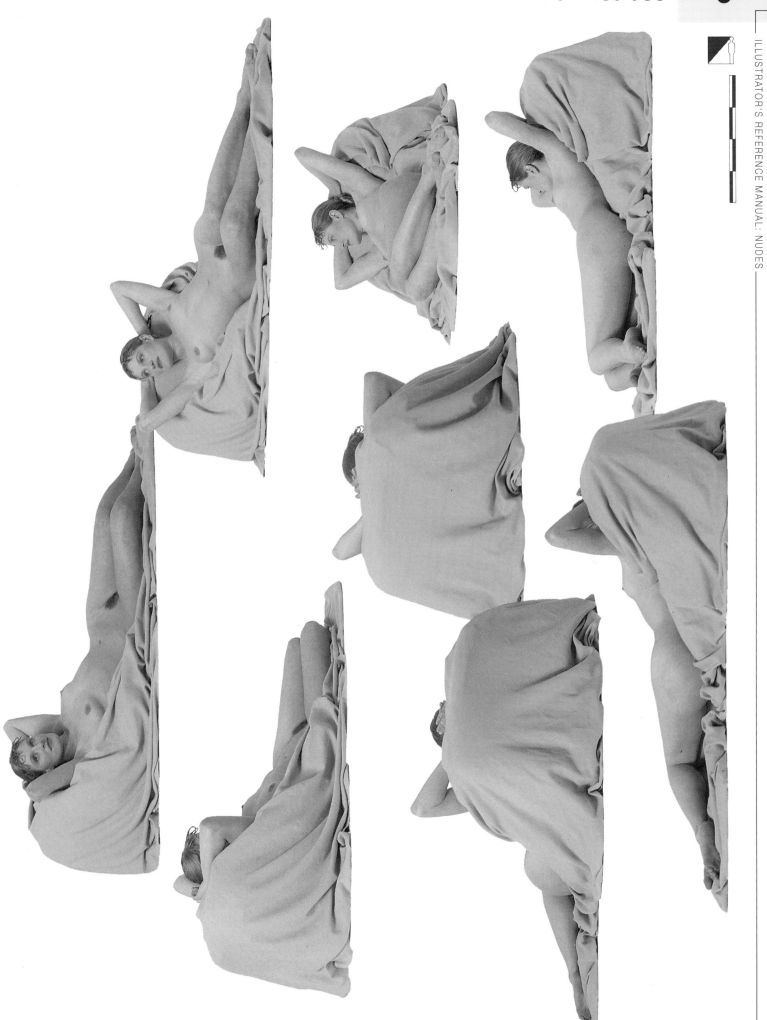

The mistress

The mistress

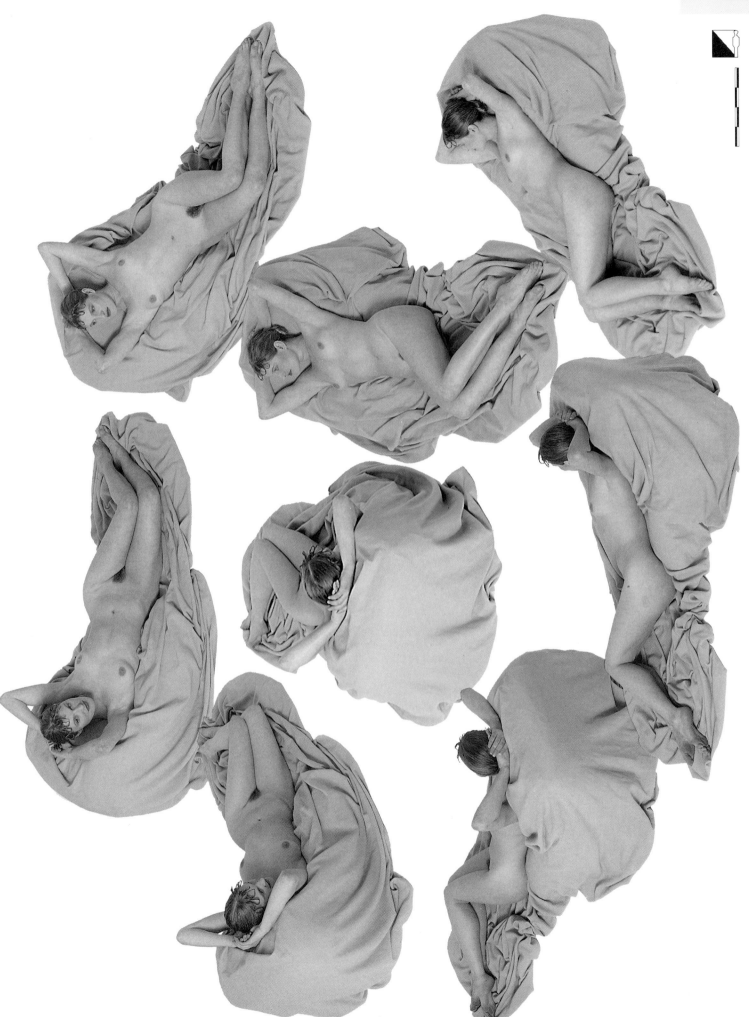

3.03

Artist's model

Artist's model

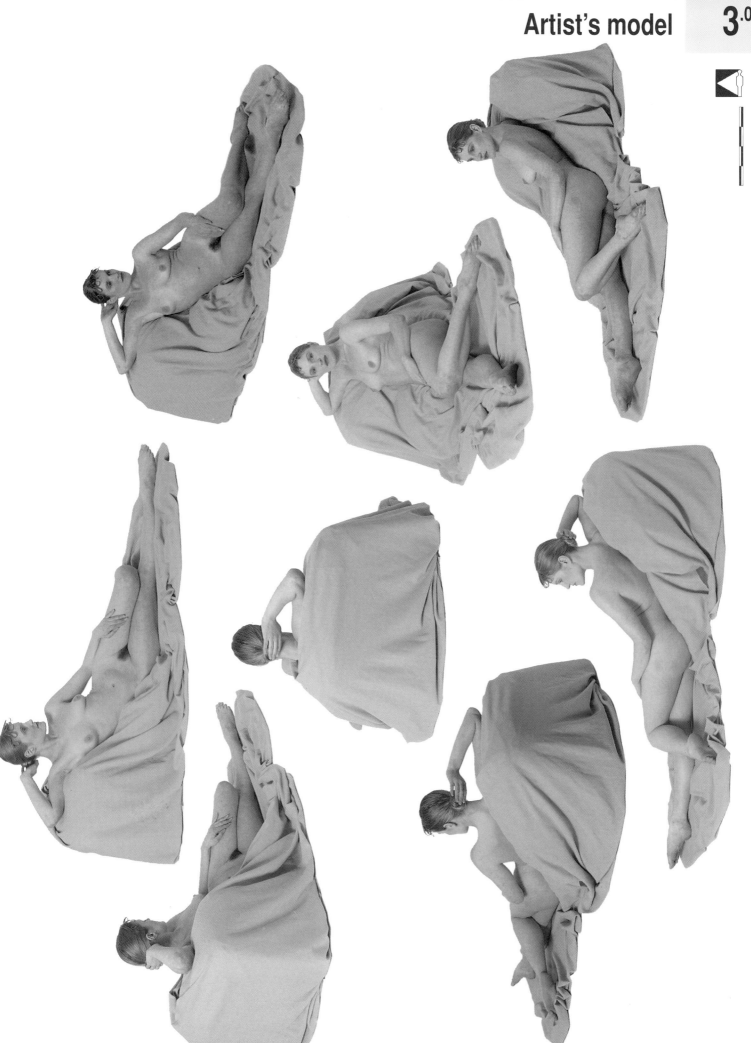

3.03

Artist's model

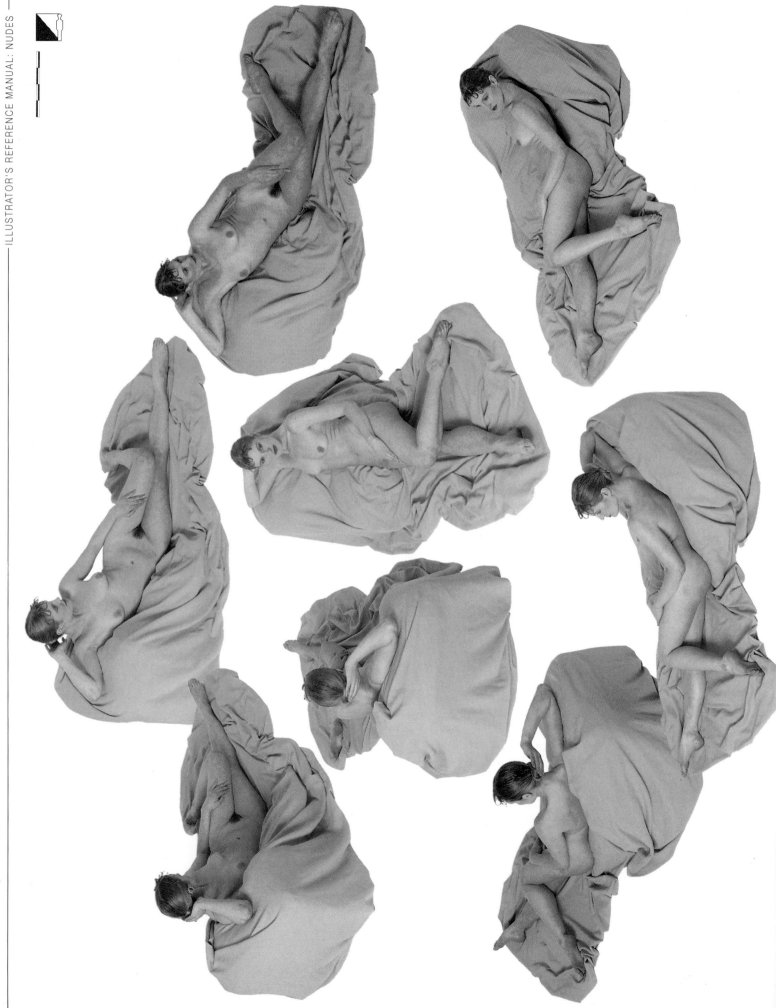

Odalisque

Odalisque

Odalisque

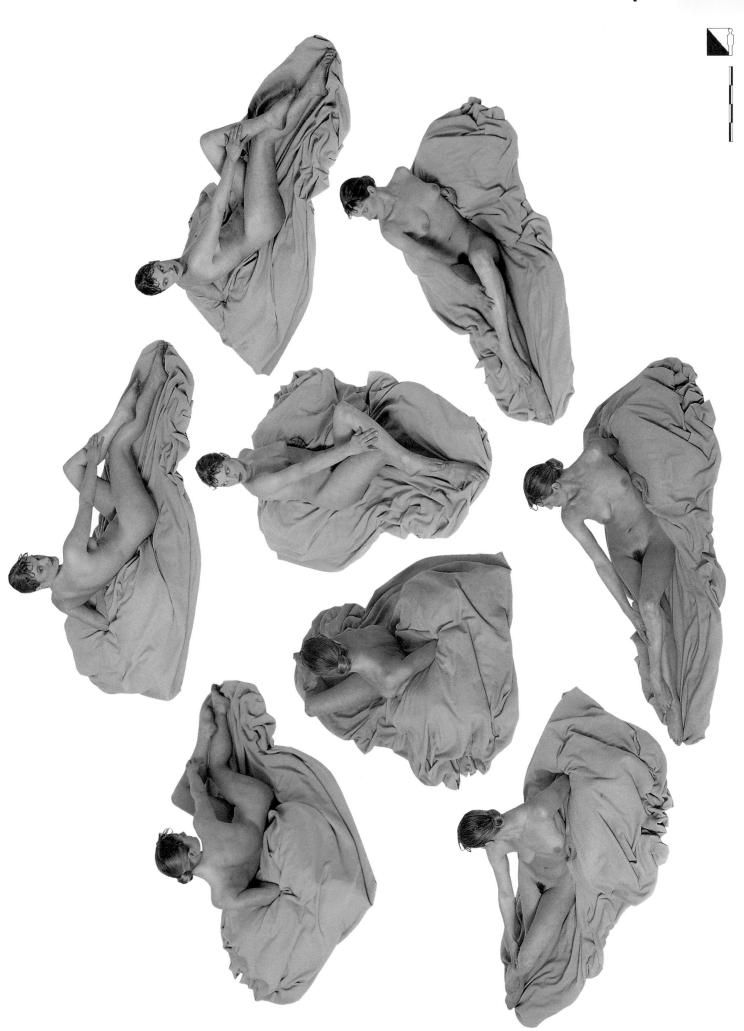

3.05

Relaxation

Relaxation

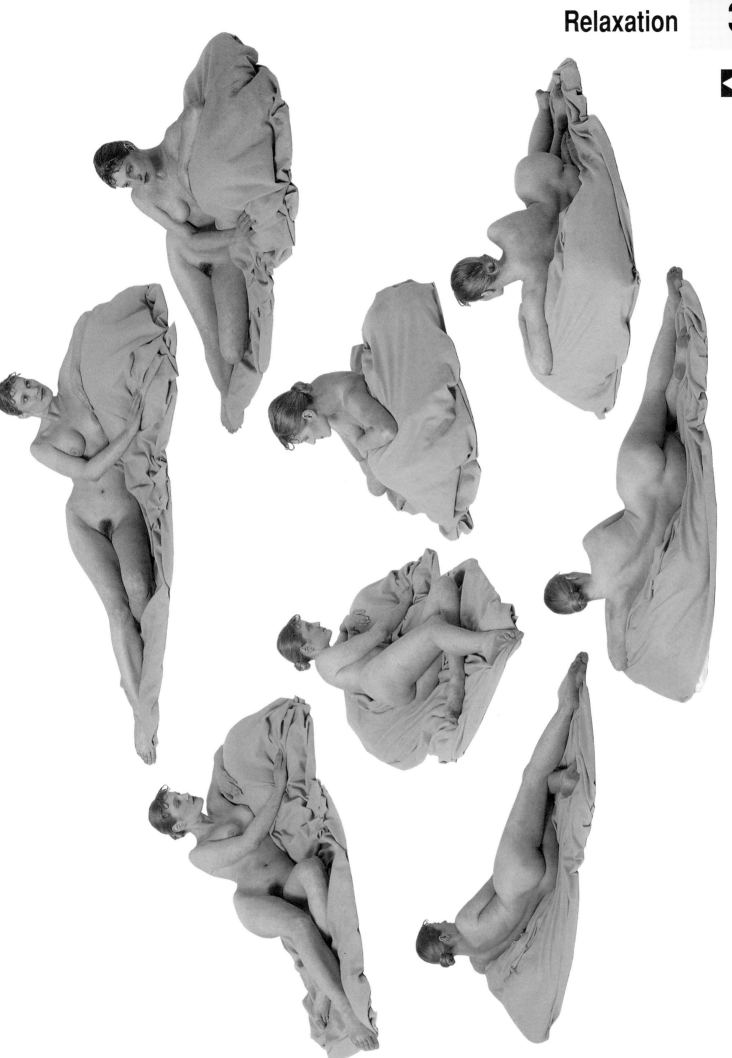

Relaxation

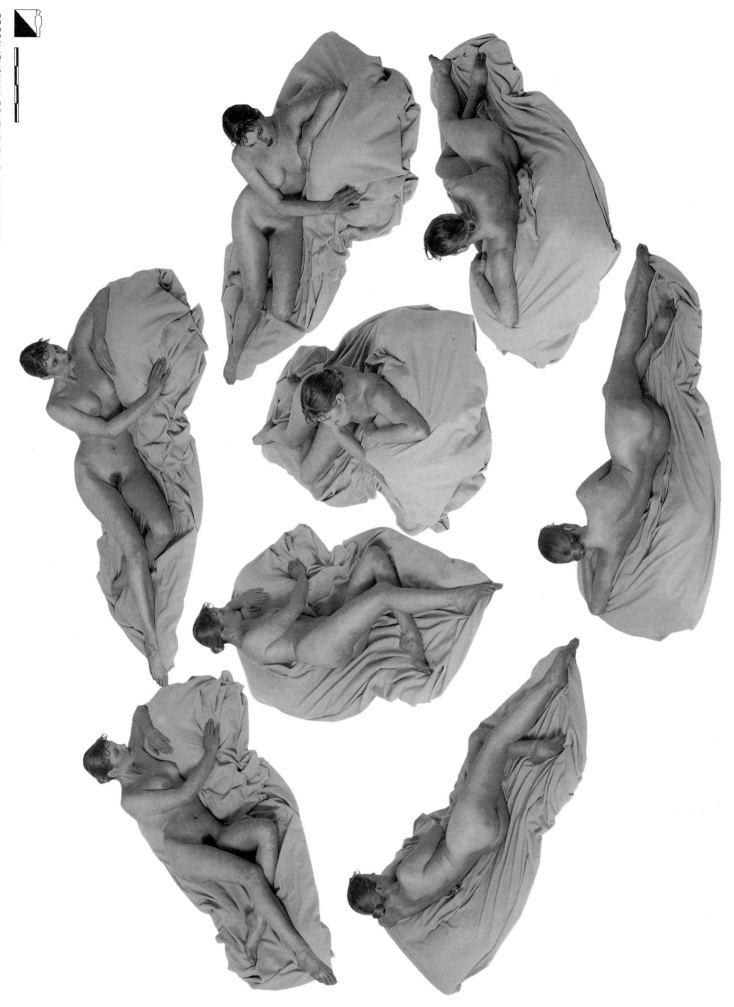

Finishing touch

Finishing touch

3.06

Finishing touch

Nymph

Nymph

Enigma

3.08

Enigma

Enigma

Invocation

Invocation

The bather

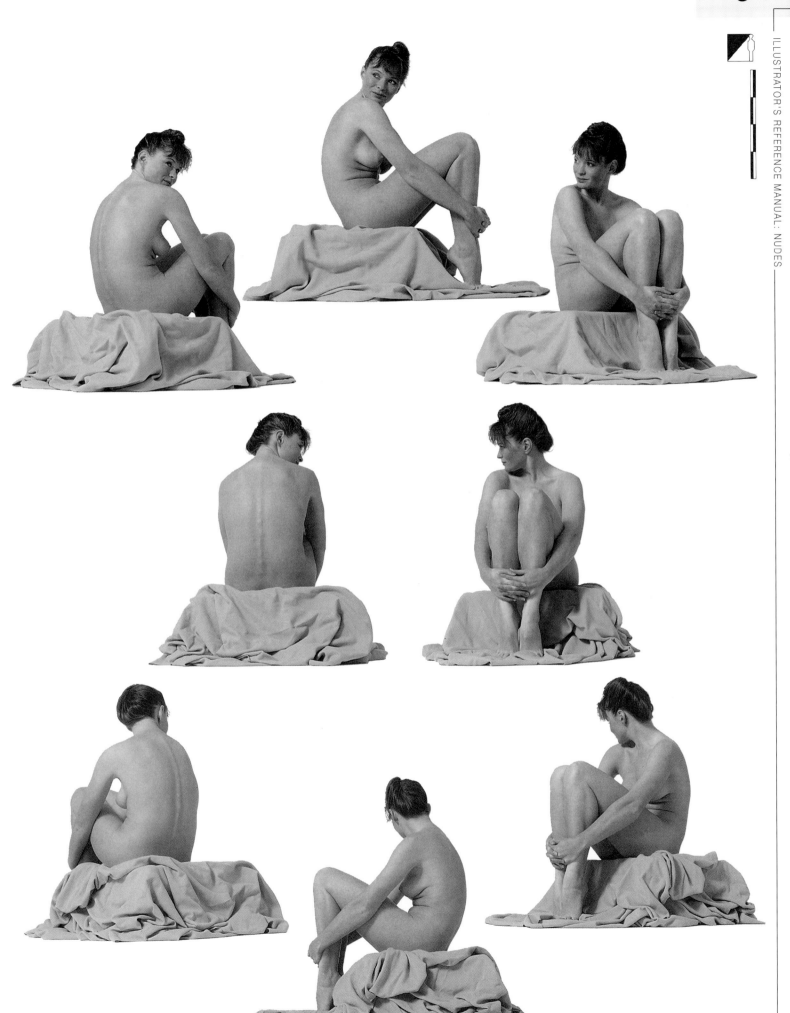

3.10

The bather

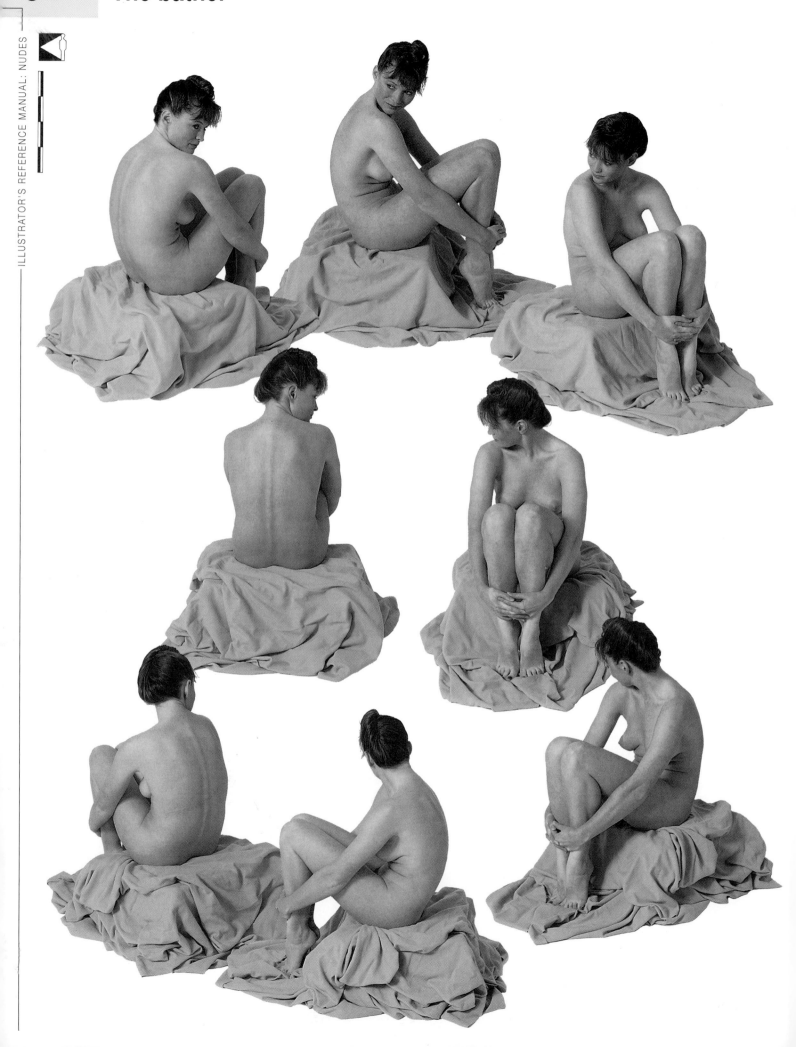

The bather

3.11 Grace

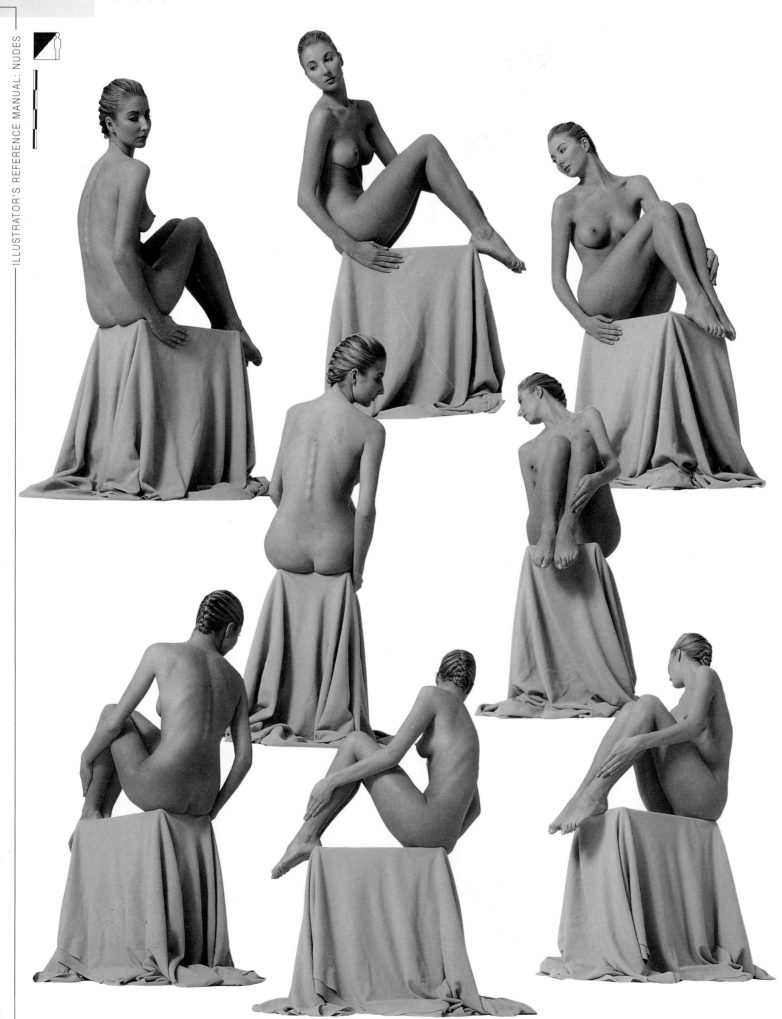

Grace

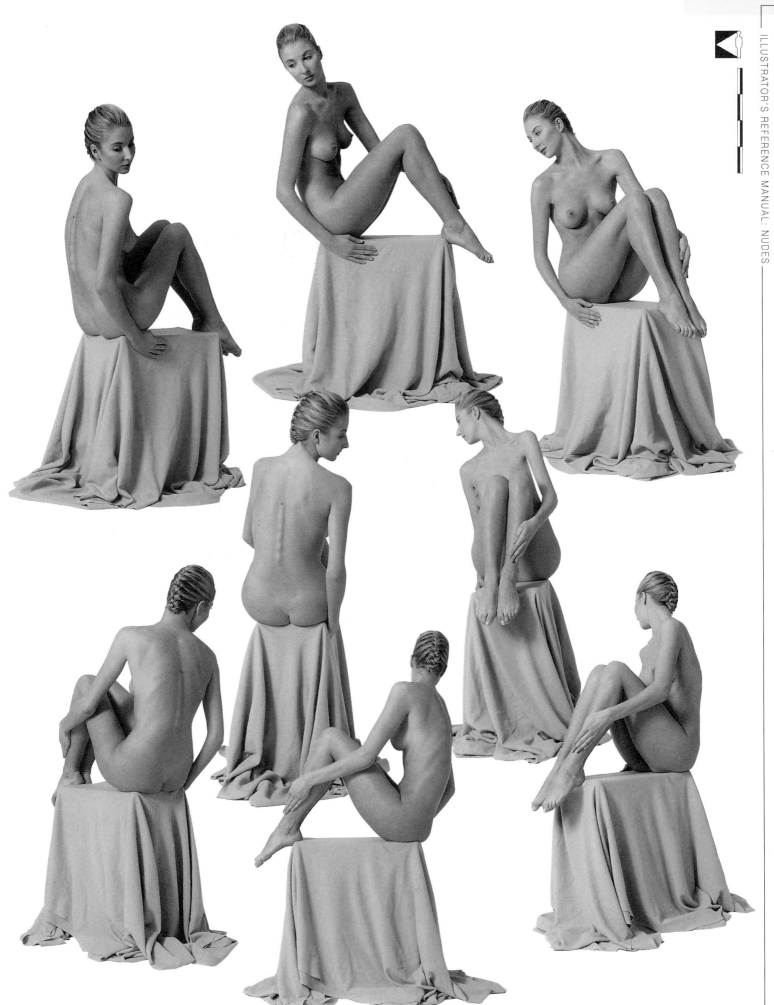

Grace

Statuesque

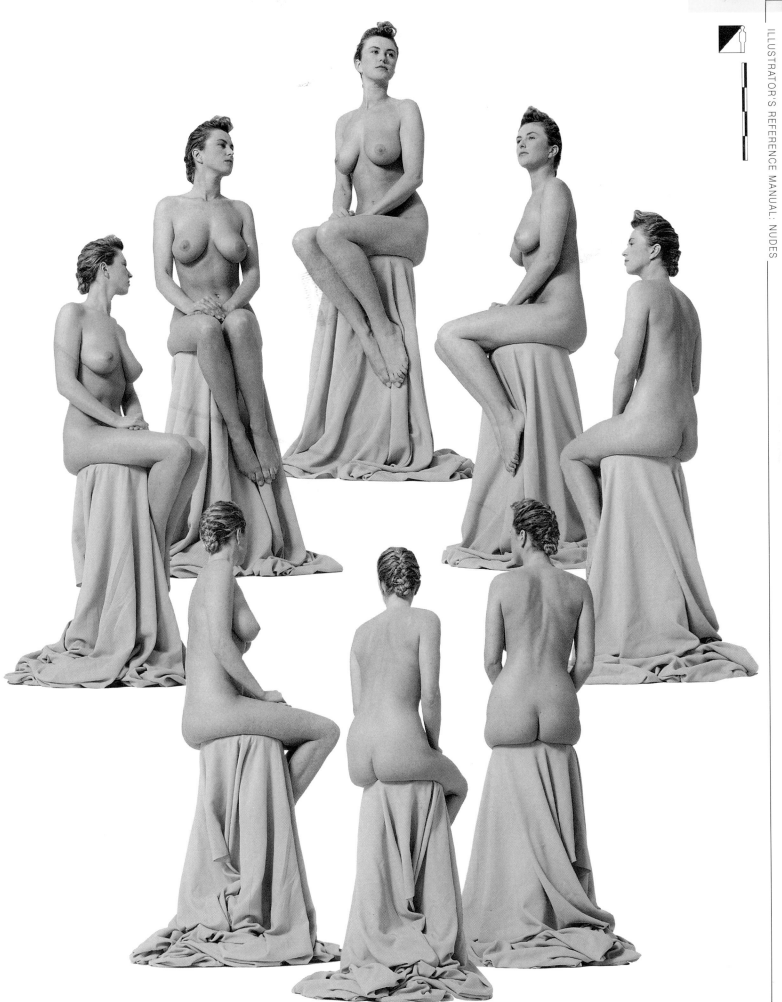

3.12

Statuesque

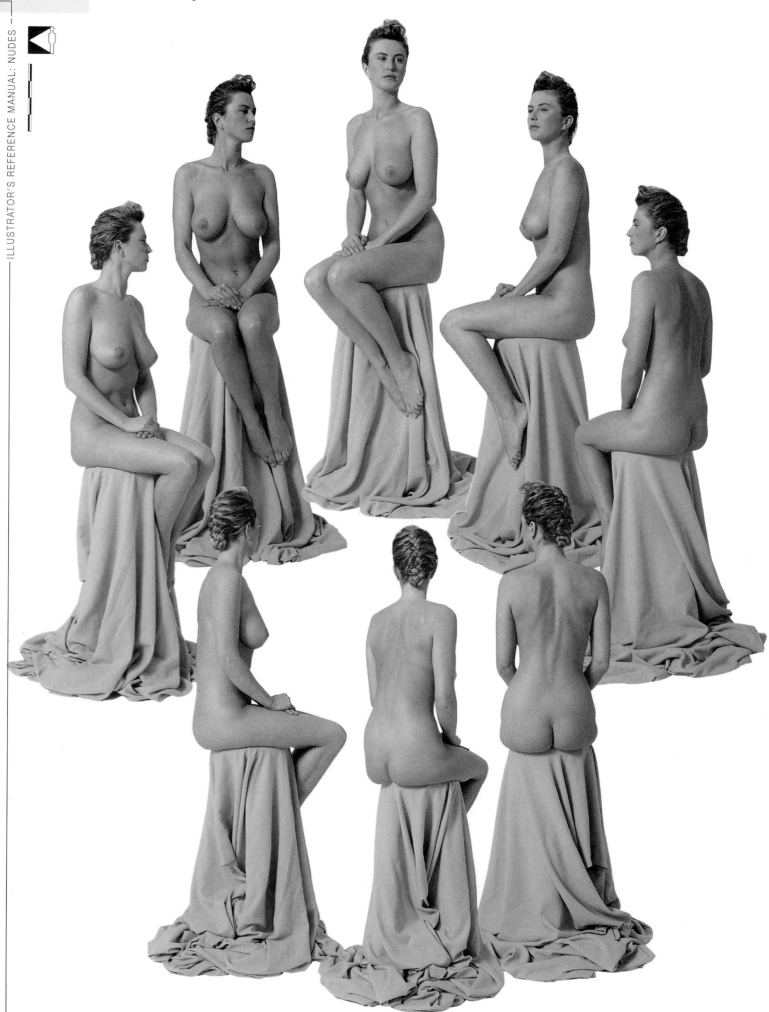

Statuesque

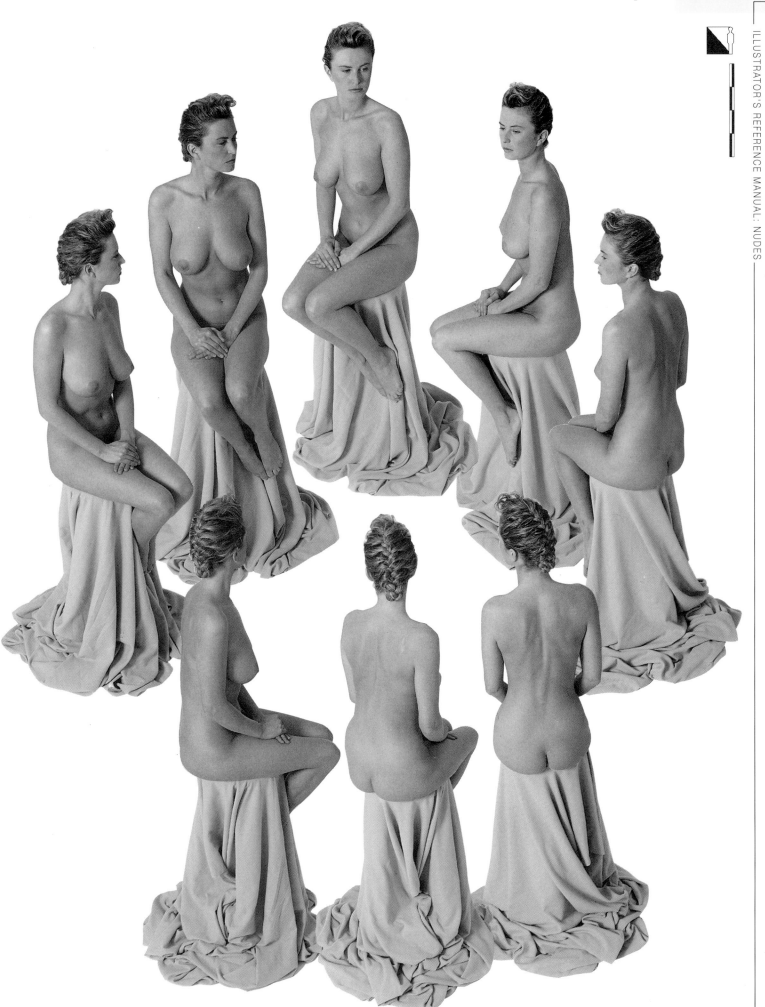

3.13

Dryad

Dryad

3.13

Dryad

The dive

3.14

The dive

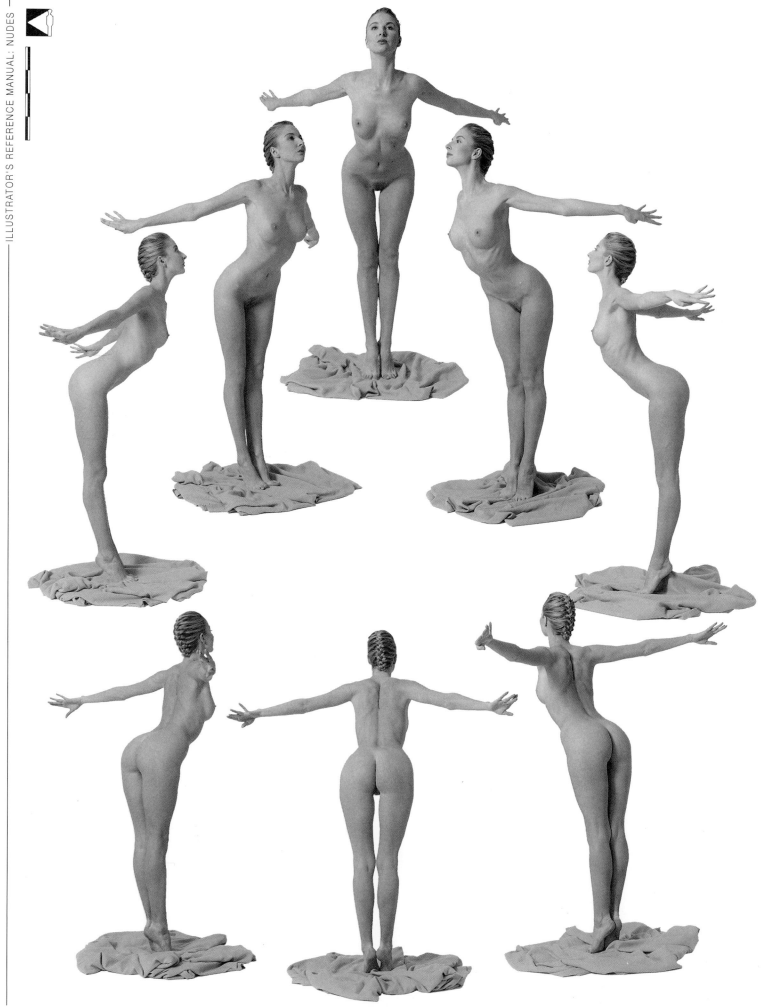

Posed

Posed

3.15

Posed

Art deco

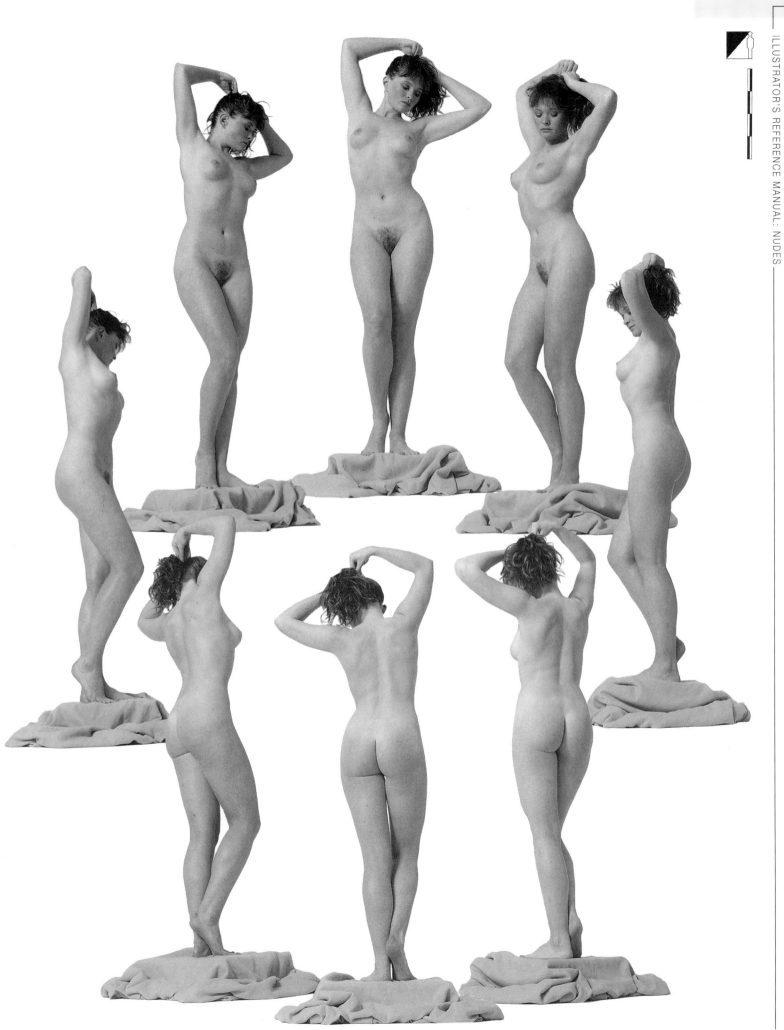

Art deco

Art deco

Elegance

Elegance

3.17

Elegance

Ballerina

Ballerina

Ballerina

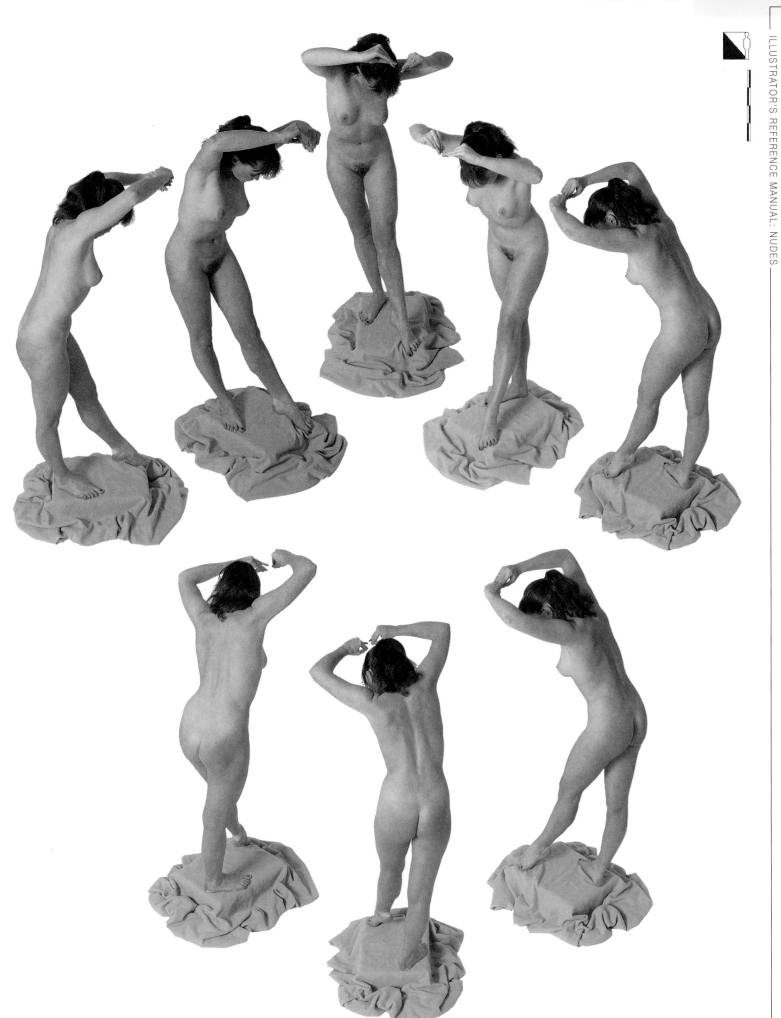

3.19

Aphrodite

Aphrodite

Aphrodite

The dying gaul

4.01

The dying gaul

The dying gaul

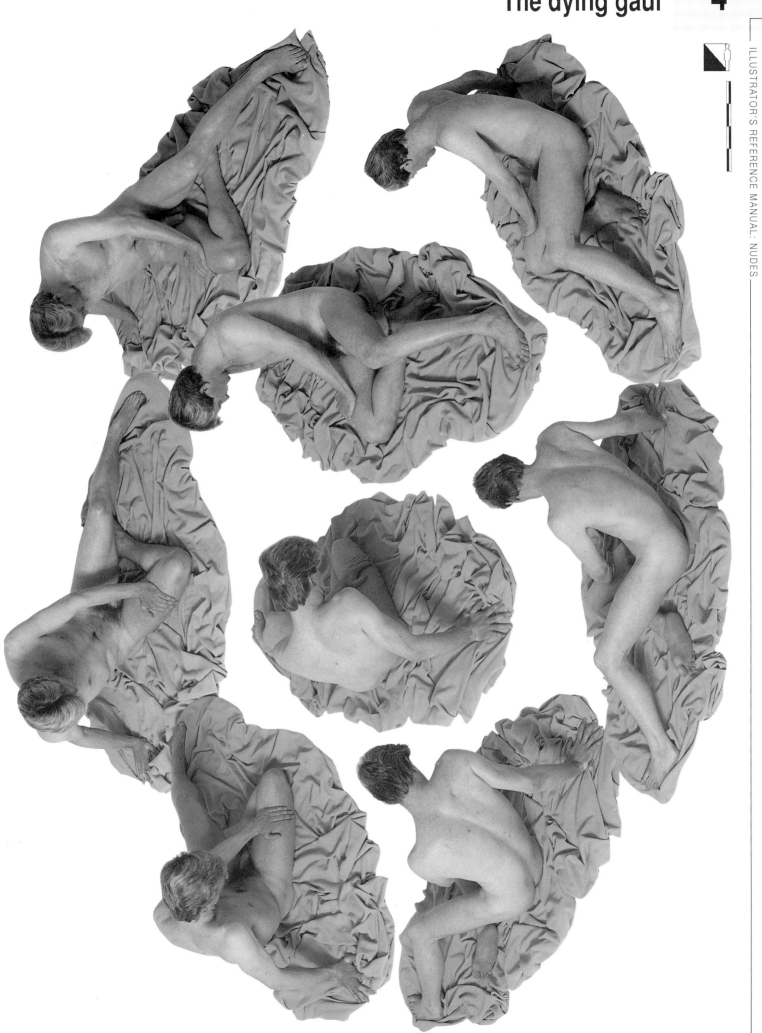

Adam

ILLUSTRATOR'S REFERENCE MANUAL: NUDES

Adam

Adam

The thinker

4.03

The thinker

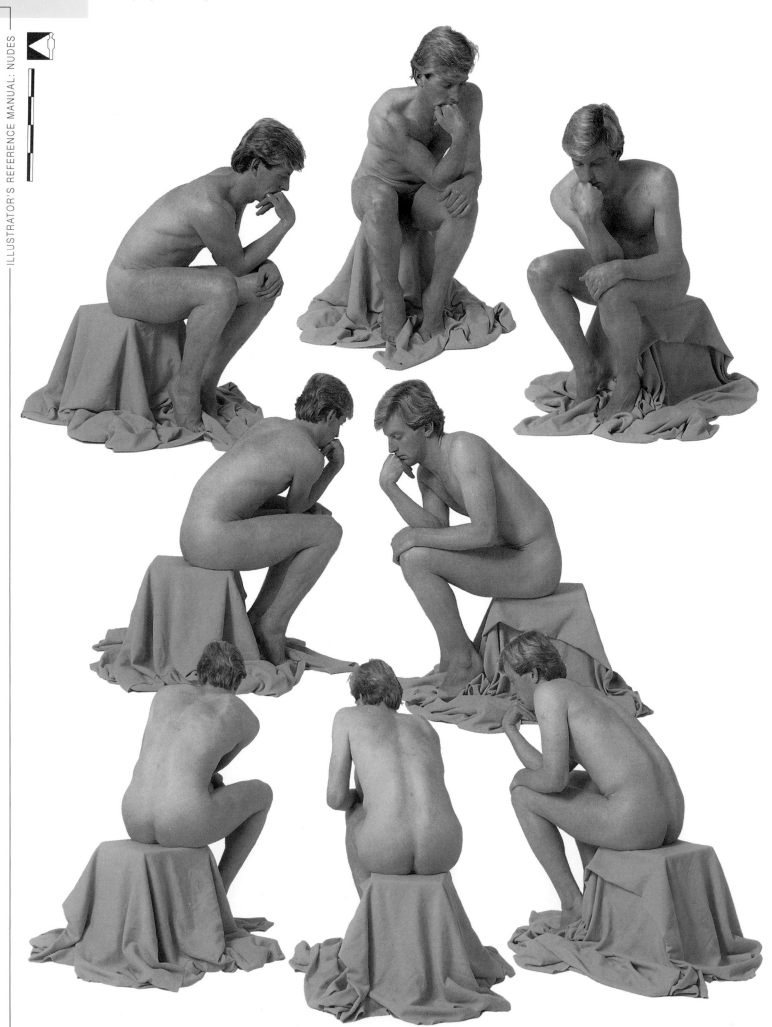

The thinker

4.04

Anguish

ILLUSTRATOR'S REFERENCE MANUAL: NUDES

Anguish

Anguish

Oedipus and the sphinx

4.05

Oedipus and the sphinx

ILLUSTRATOR'S REFERENCE MANUAL: NUDES

Oedipus and the sphinx

4.06

Shotput

Shotput

4.06

Shotput

The discus thrower

The discus thrower

The discus thrower

Abandon

Abandon

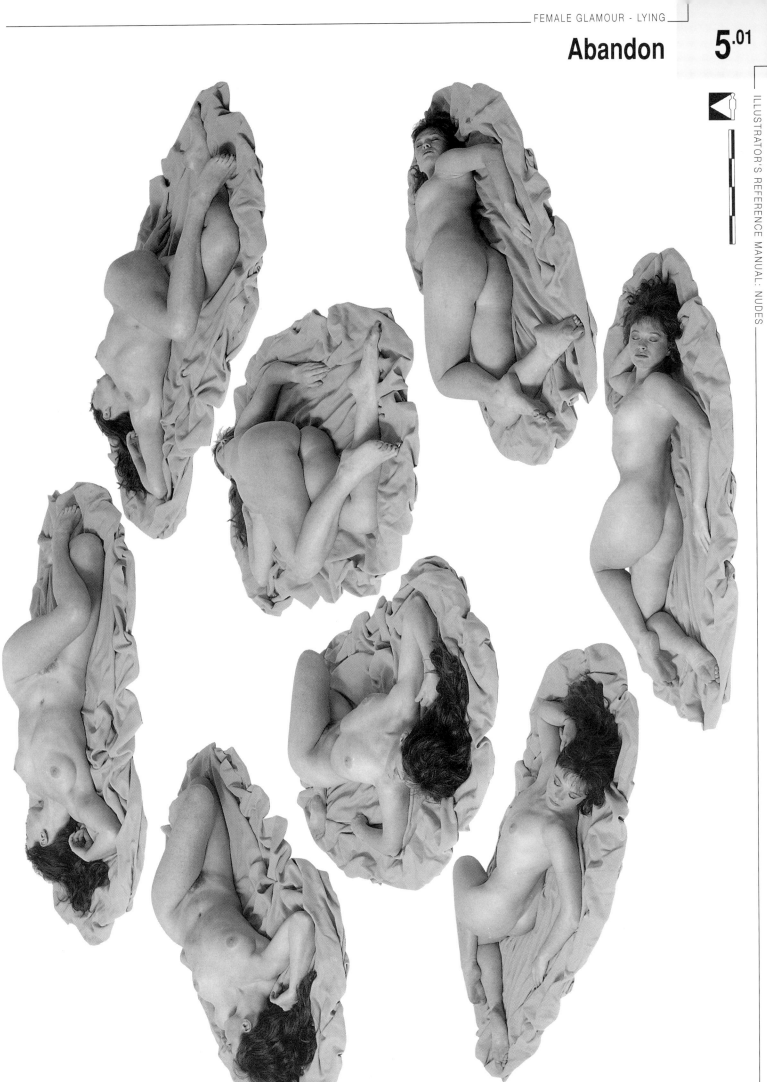

5.01

Abandon

Sultry

Sultry

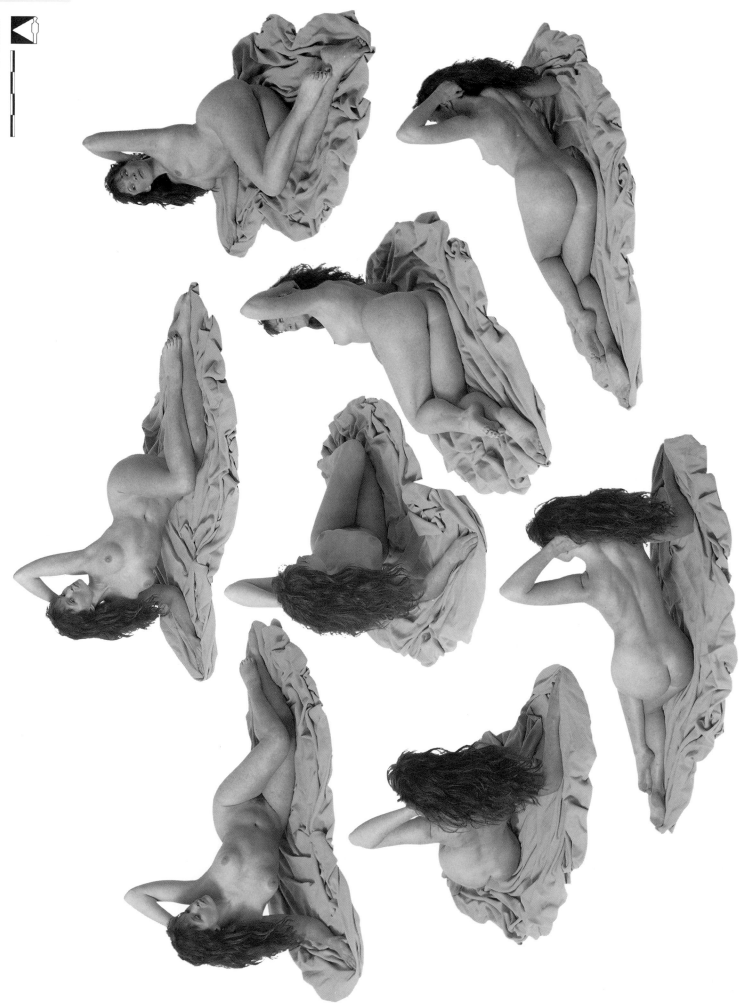

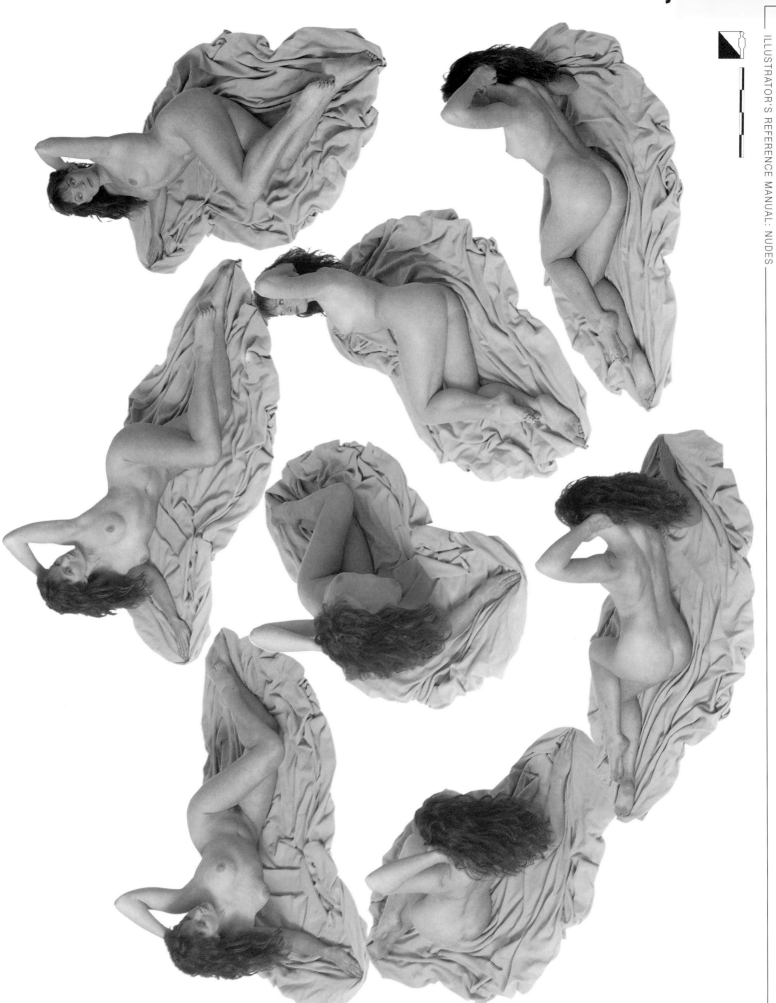

5.03

Vamp

Vamp

Vamp

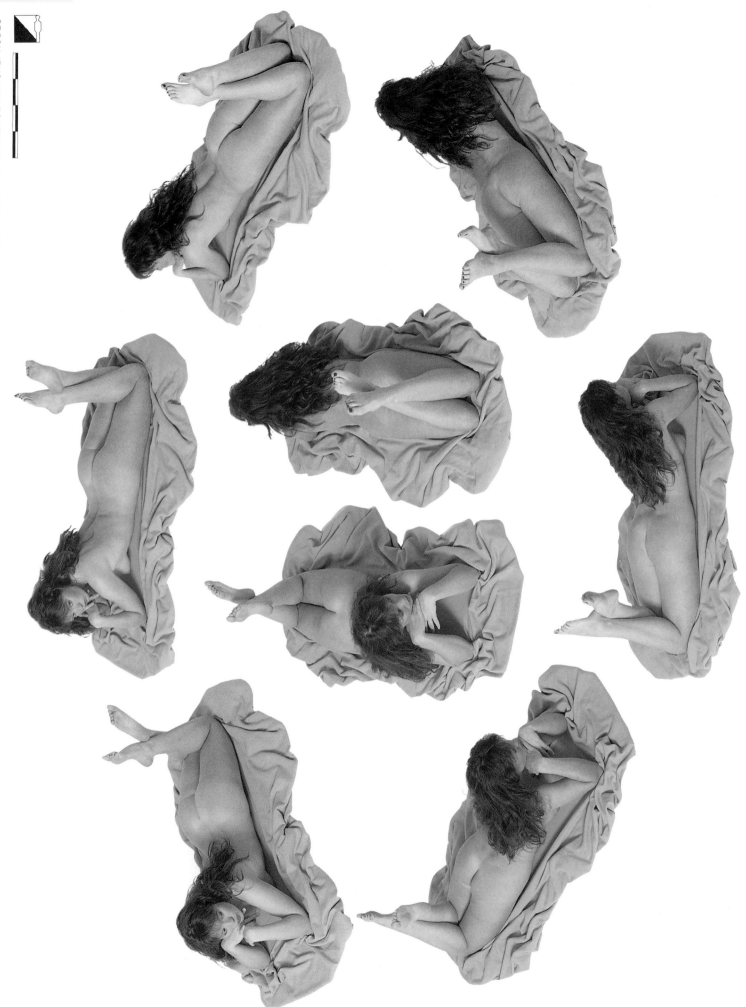

Sex kitten

Sex kitten

Sex kitten

5.05 Calendar girl

Calendar girl

5.05

Calendar girl

Temptress

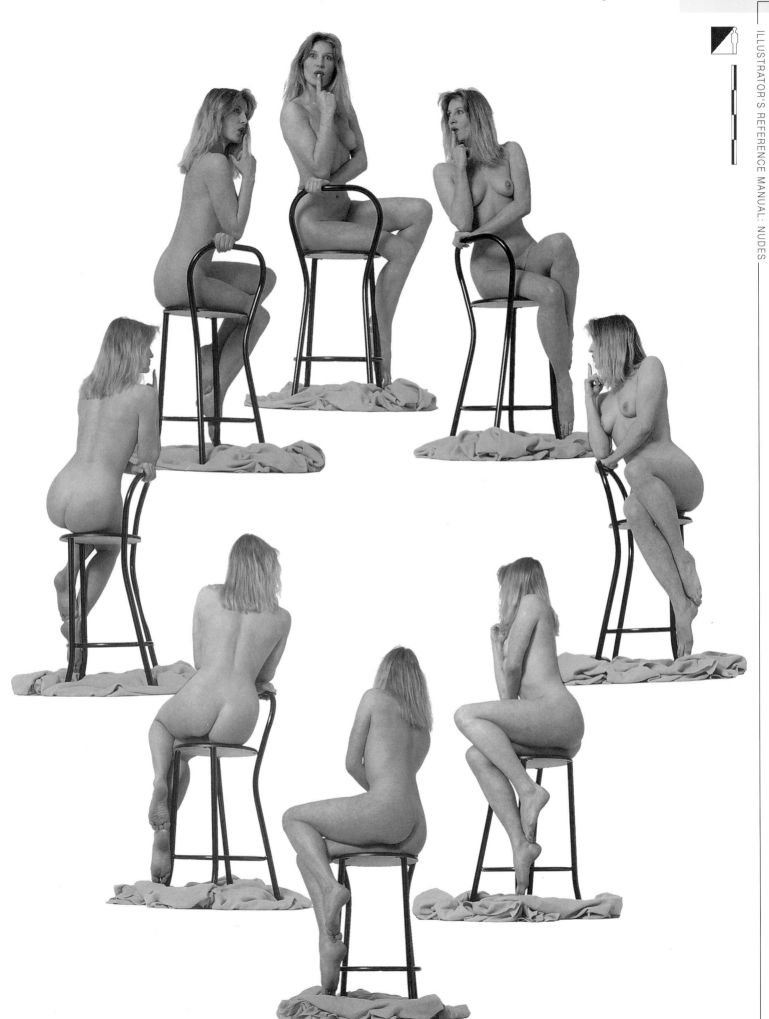

Temptress

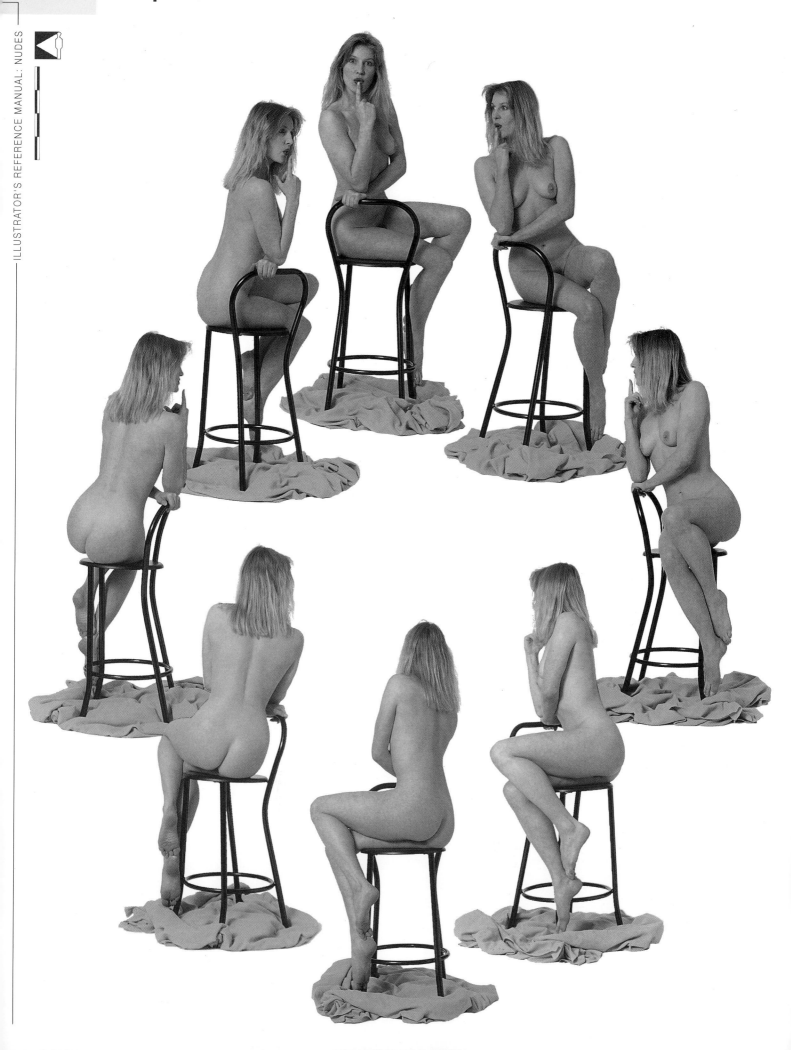

Temptress

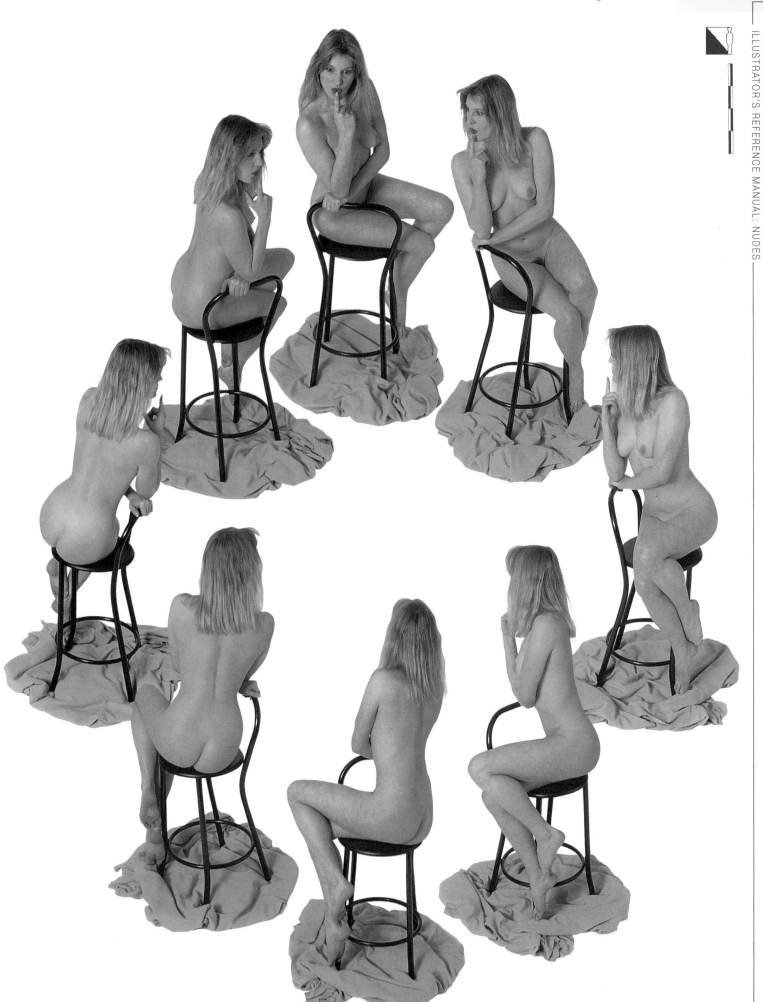

Center spread

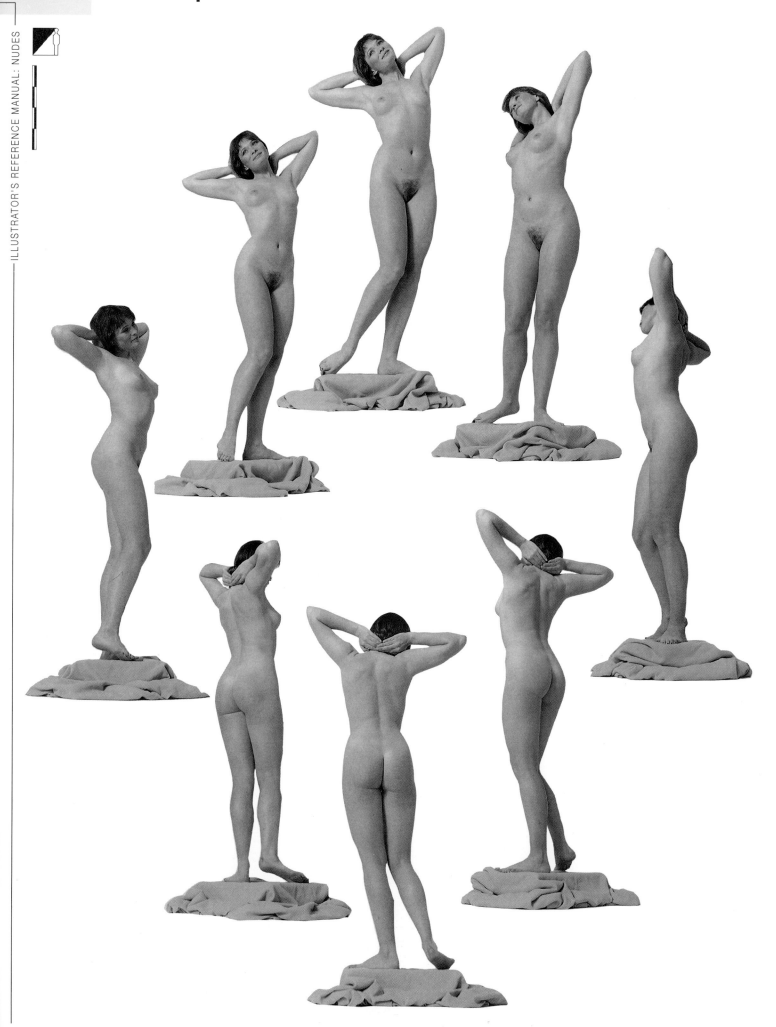

Center spread

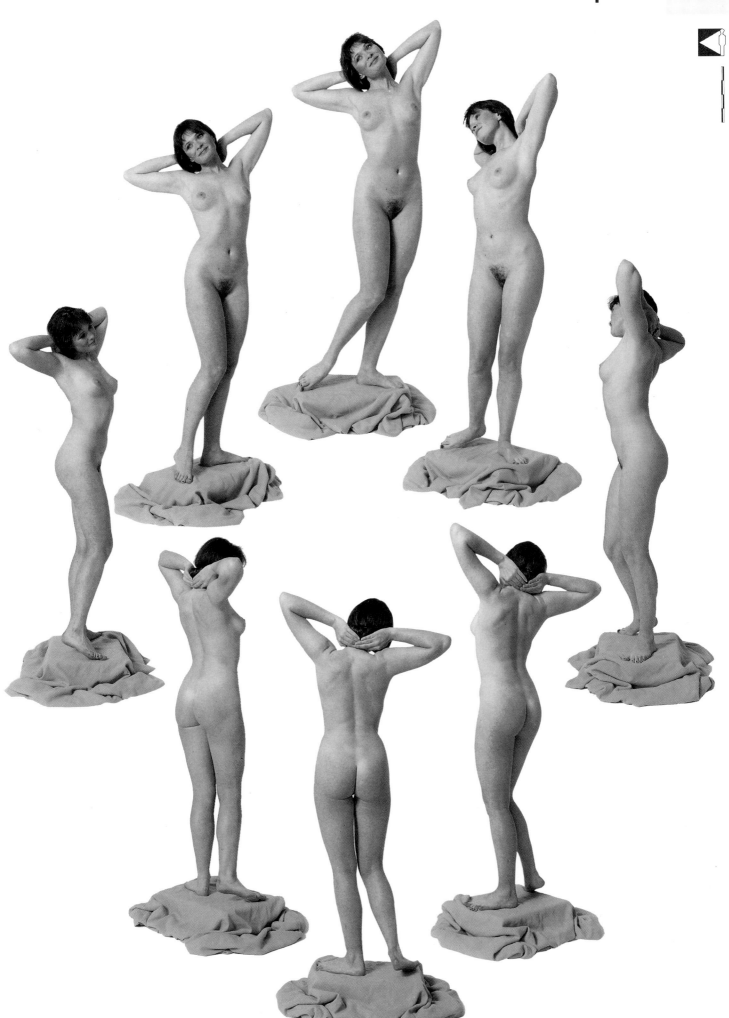

5.07

Center spread

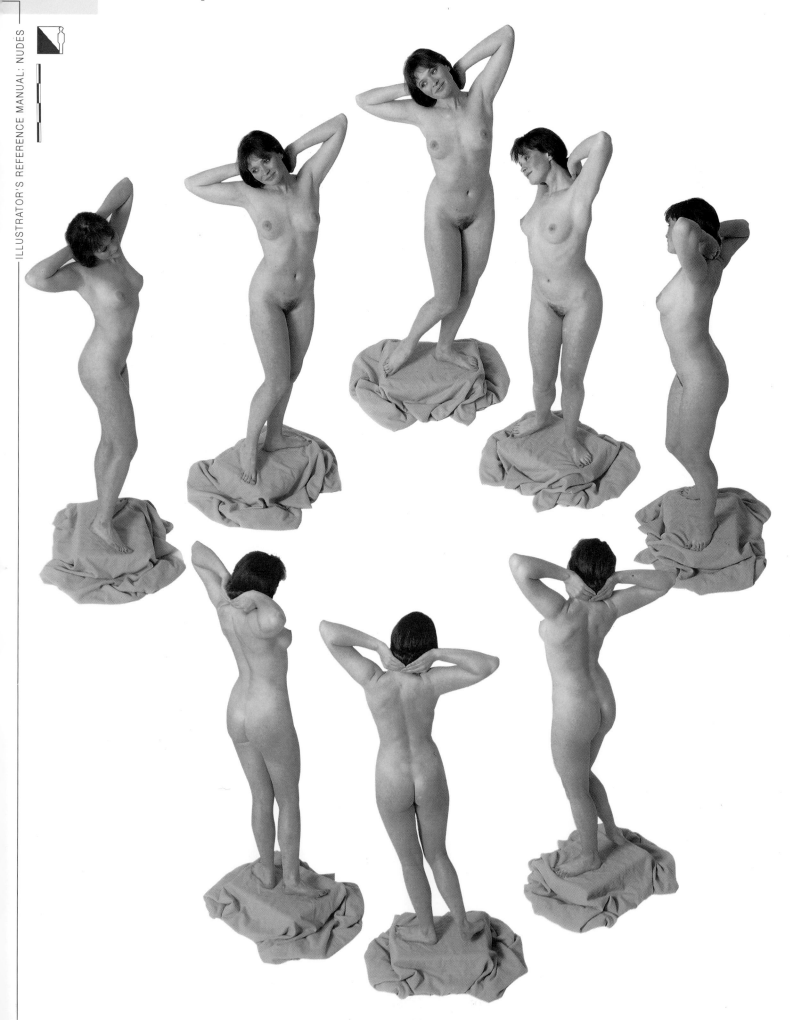

Hi there!

5.08

Hi there!

6.01

Abandon

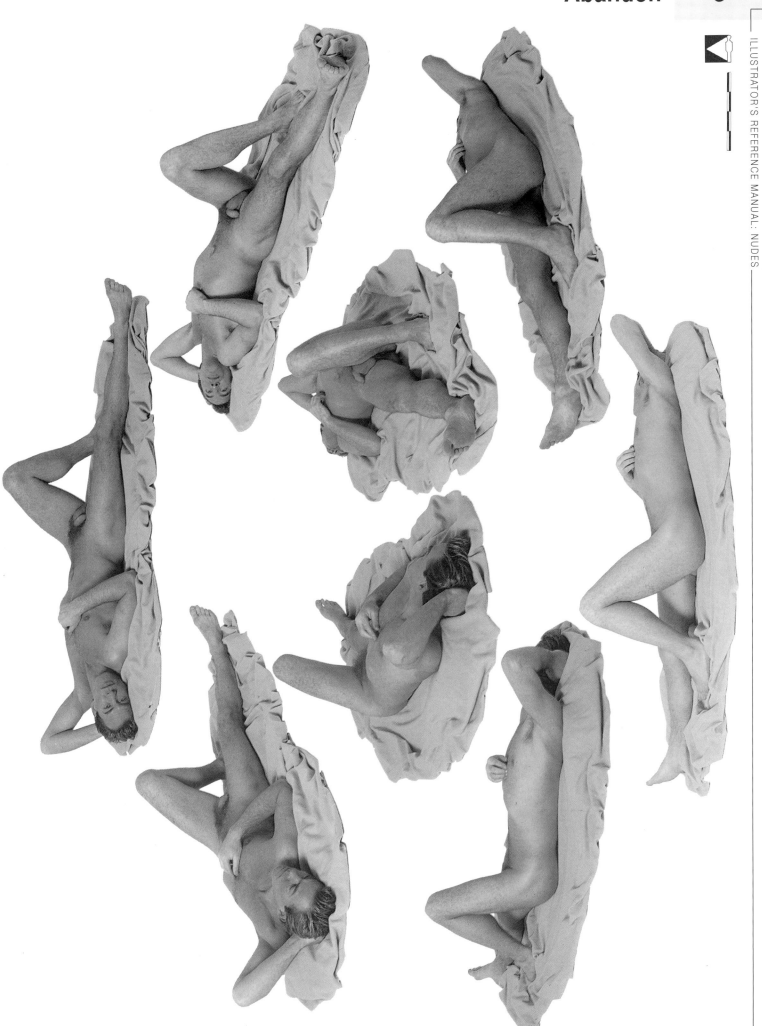

6.01

Abandon

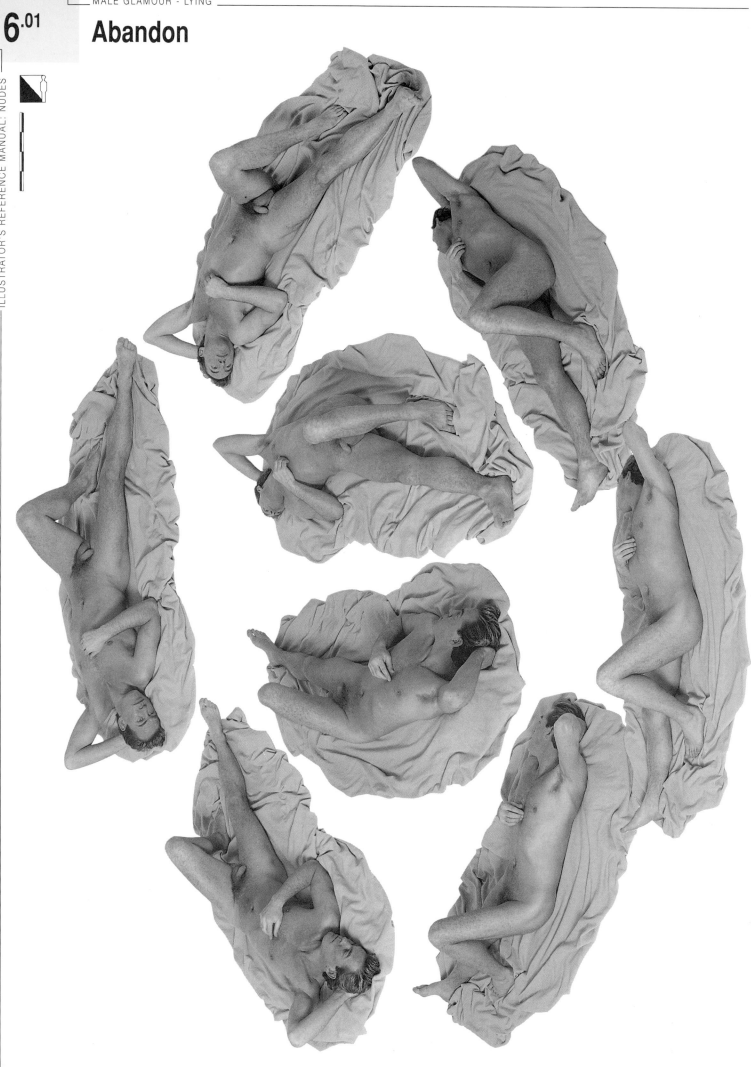

Pin-up

6.02

Pin-up

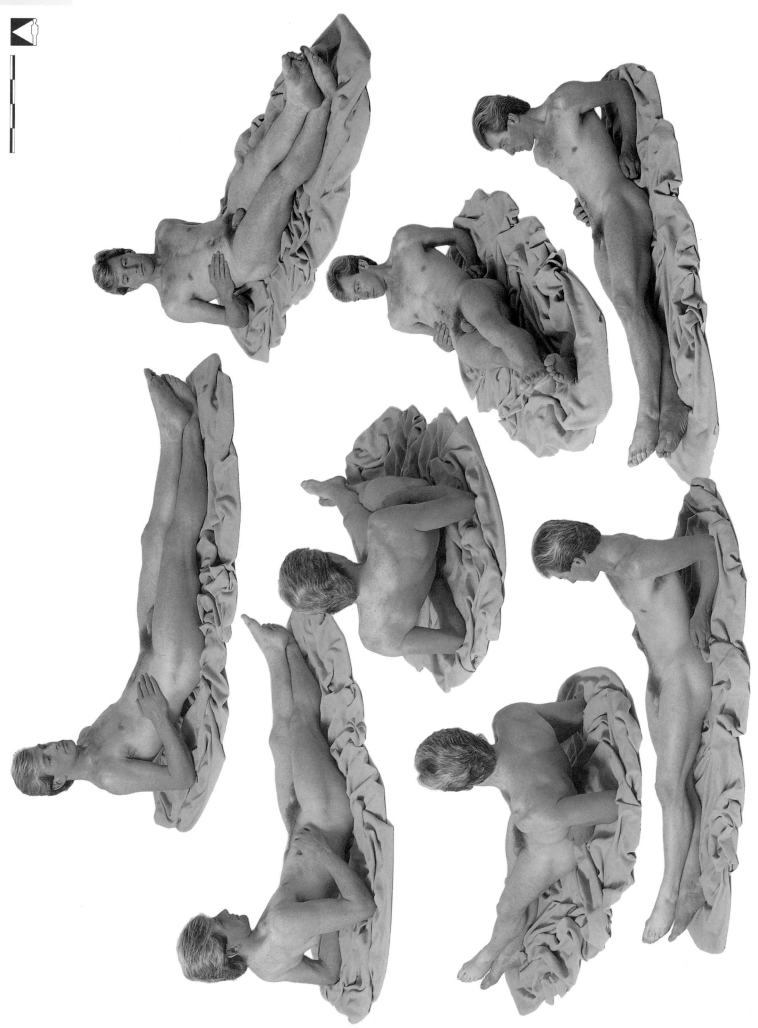

Pin-up

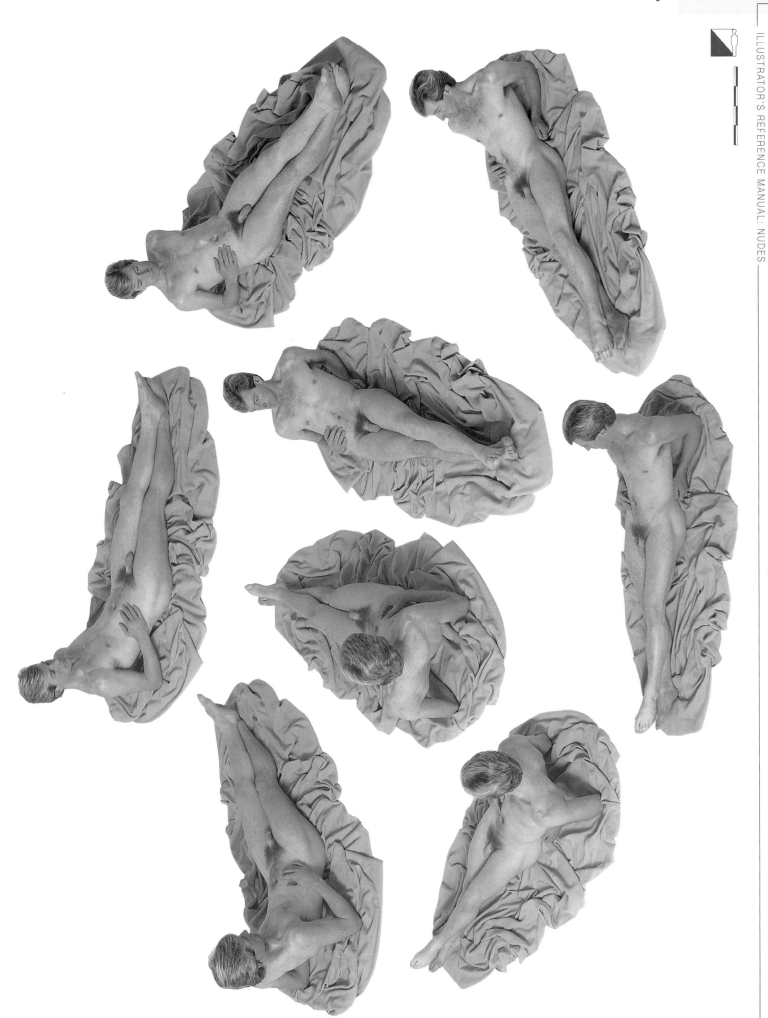

Playmate

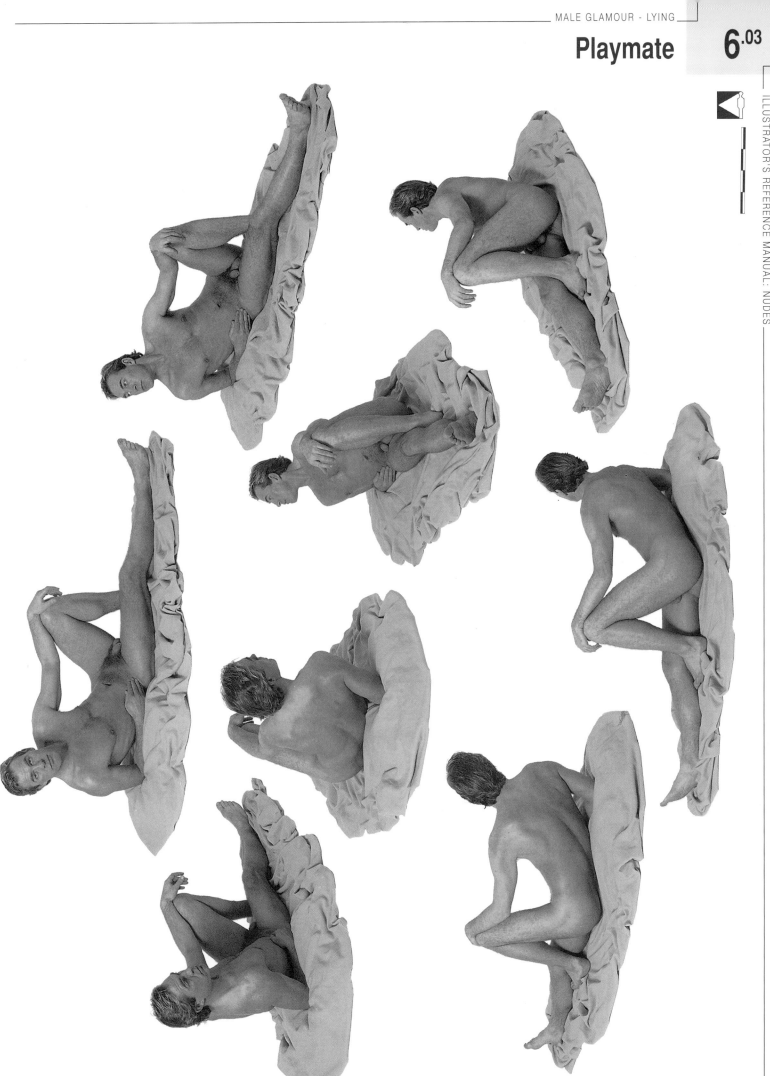

Playmate

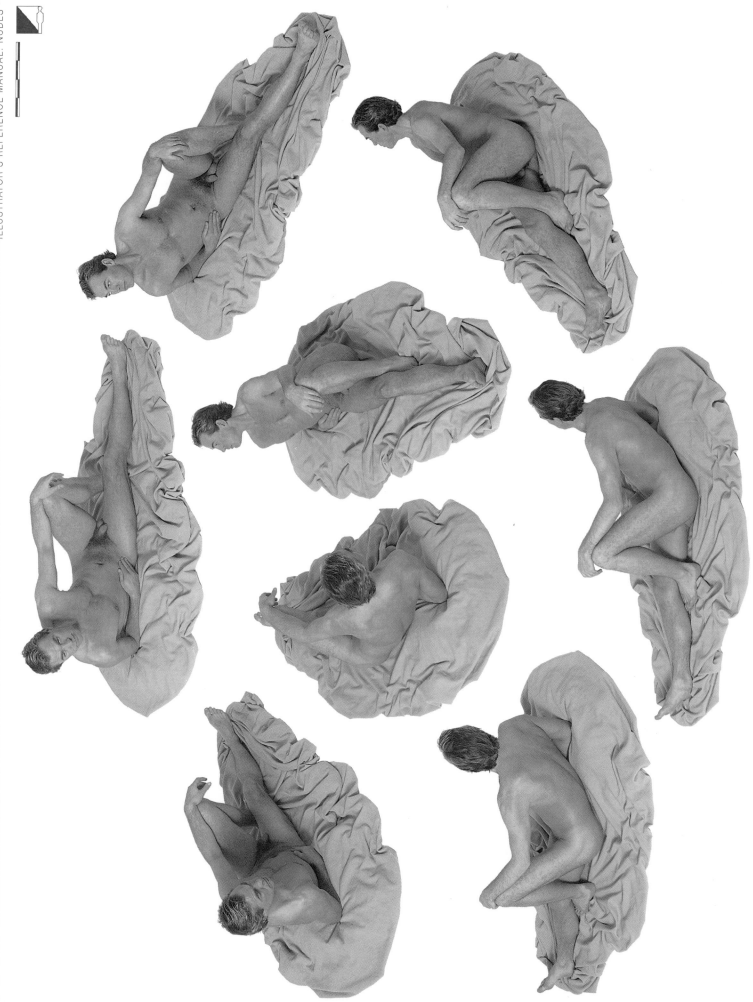

The sleep

7.01

The sleep

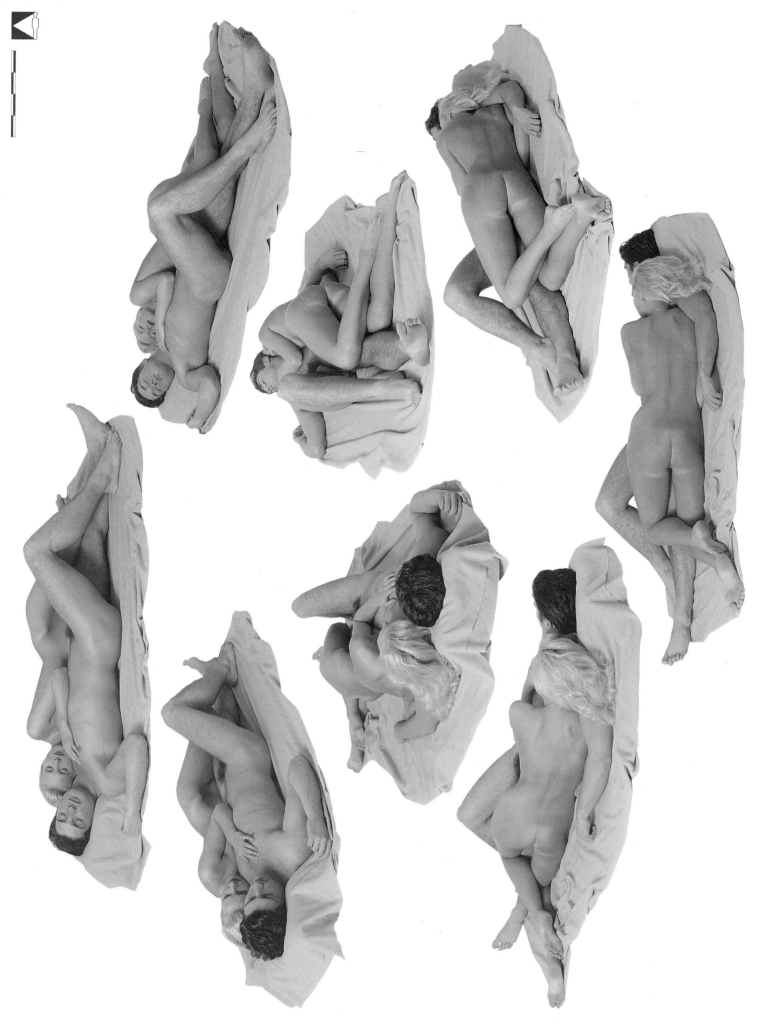

The sleep

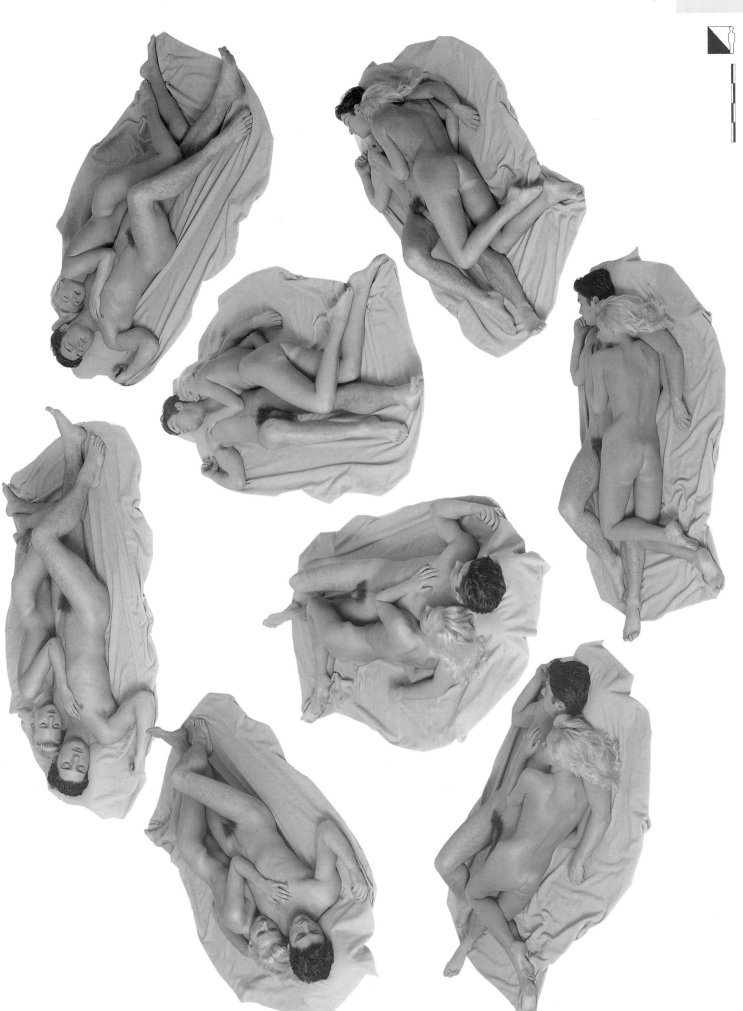

Affection

Affection

7.02

Affection

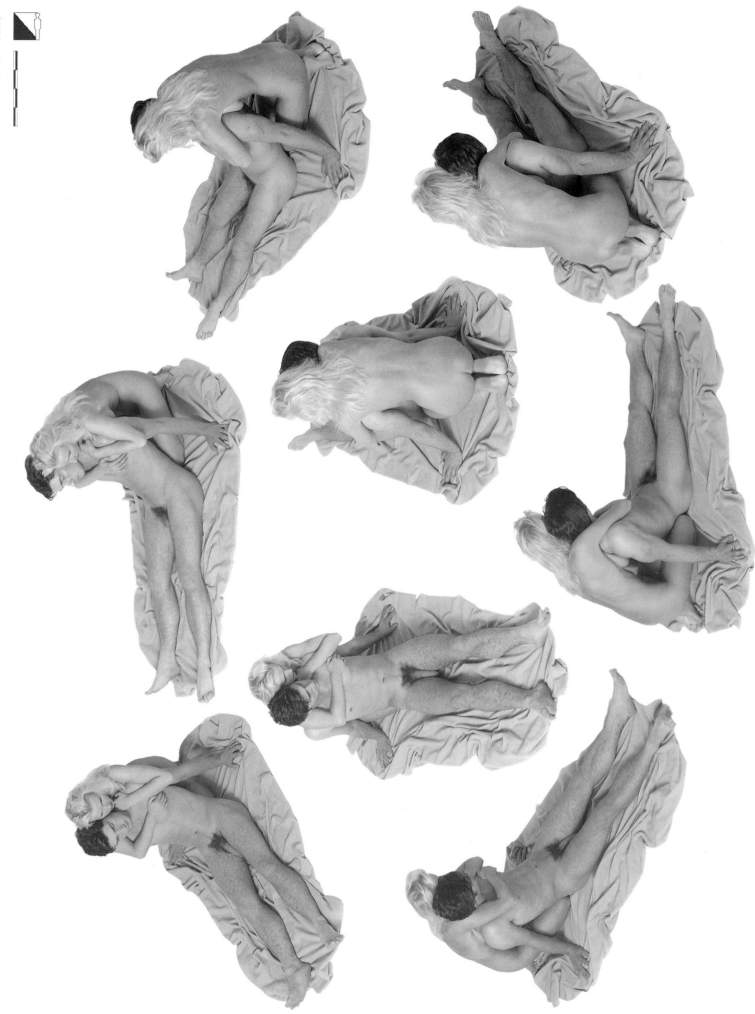

Intimacy

Intimacy

Intimacy

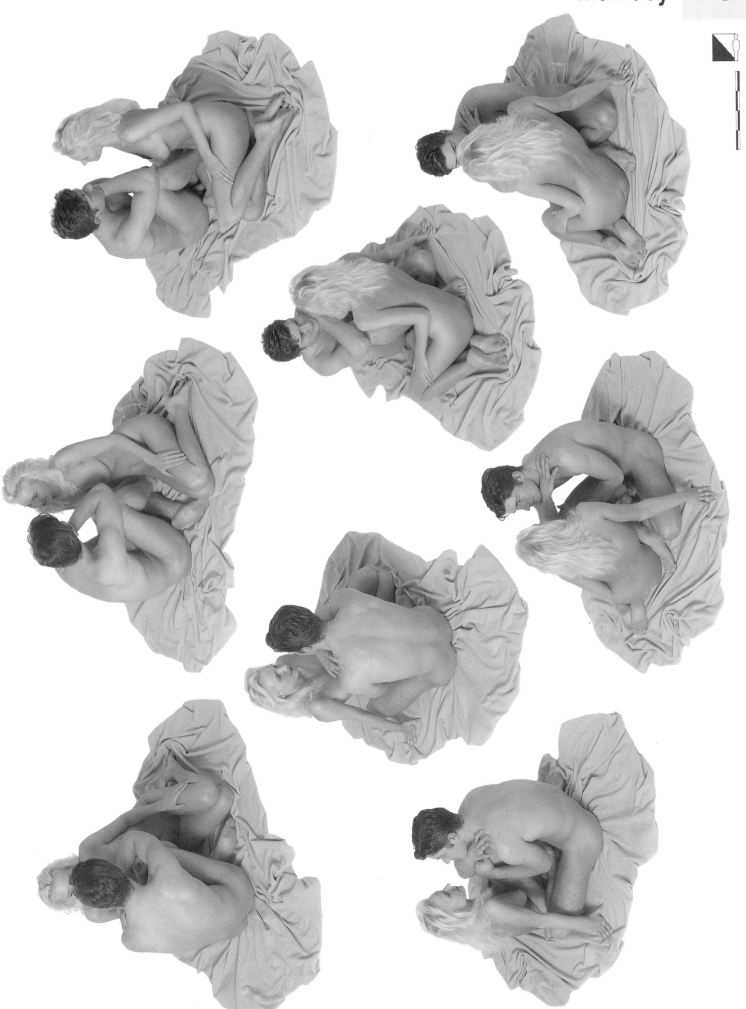

Tenderness

Tenderness

Tenderness

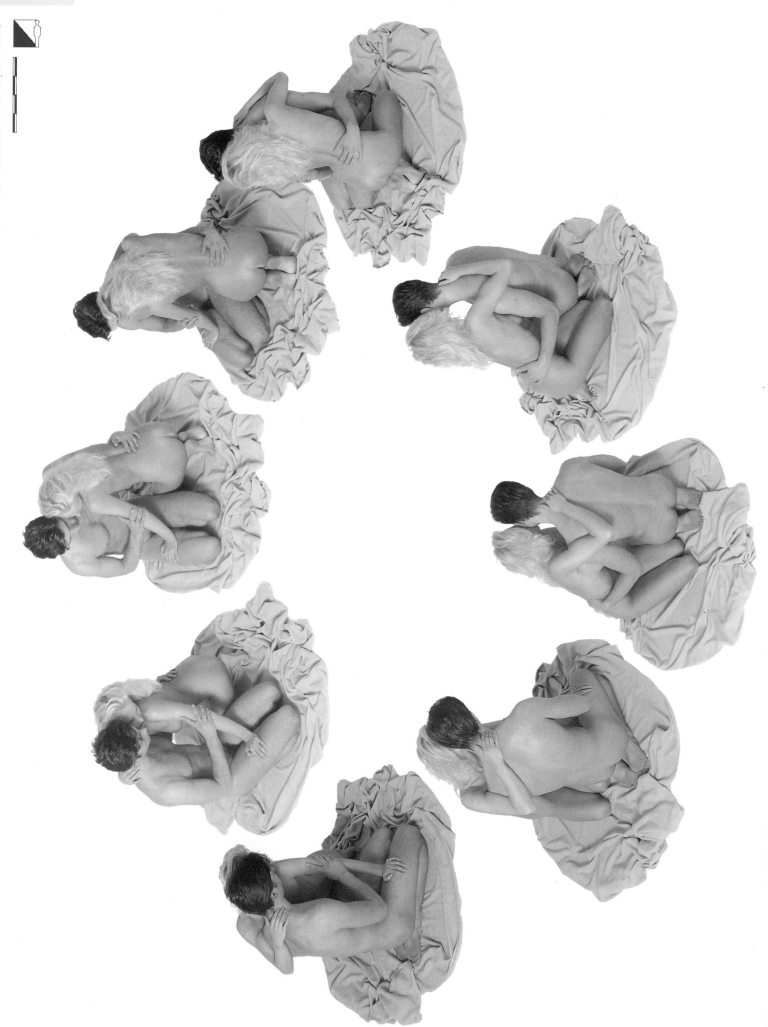

The kiss

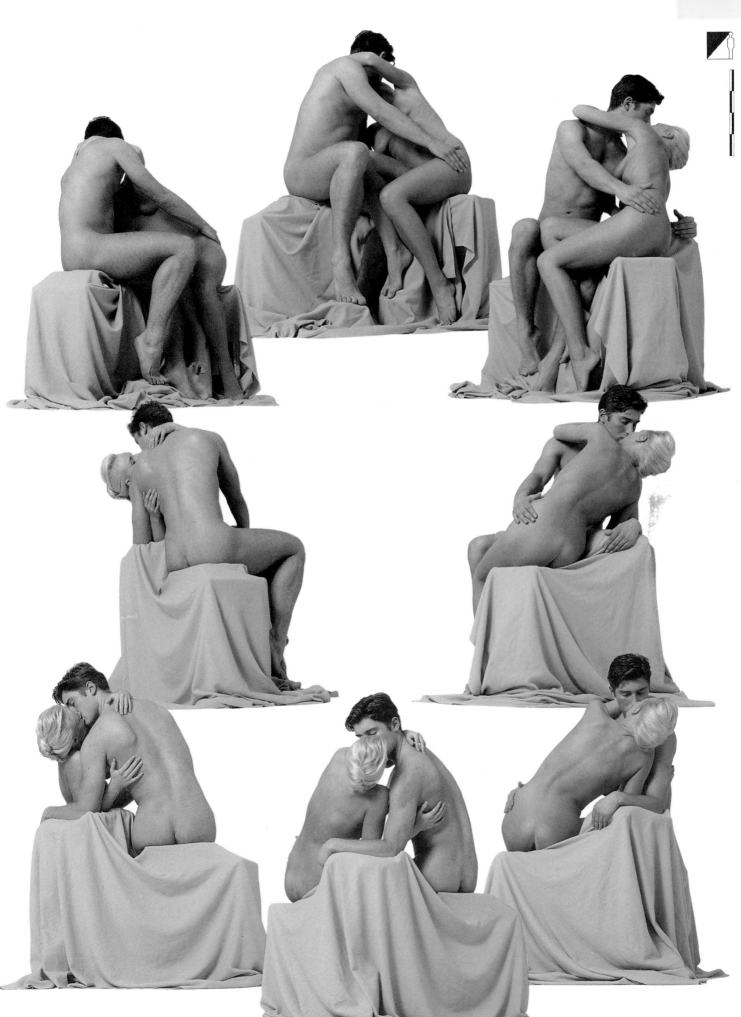

7.05

The kiss

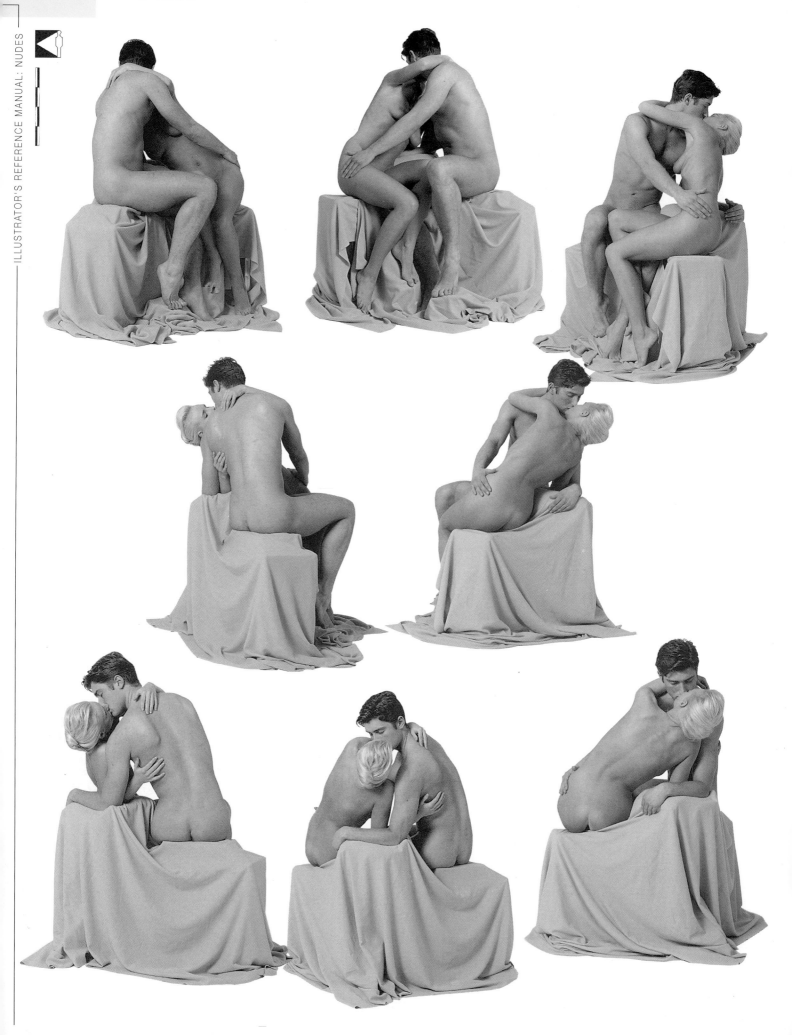

The kiss

The dance

7.06

The dance

7.07

The embrace

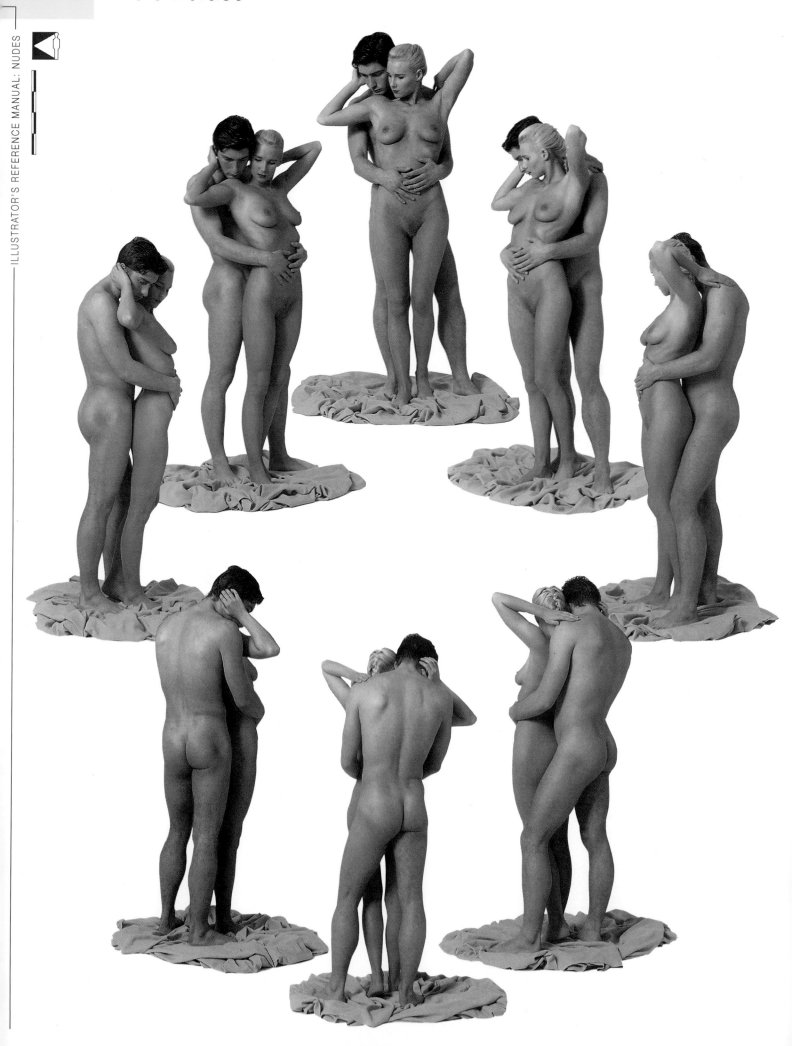

7.08

Innocence

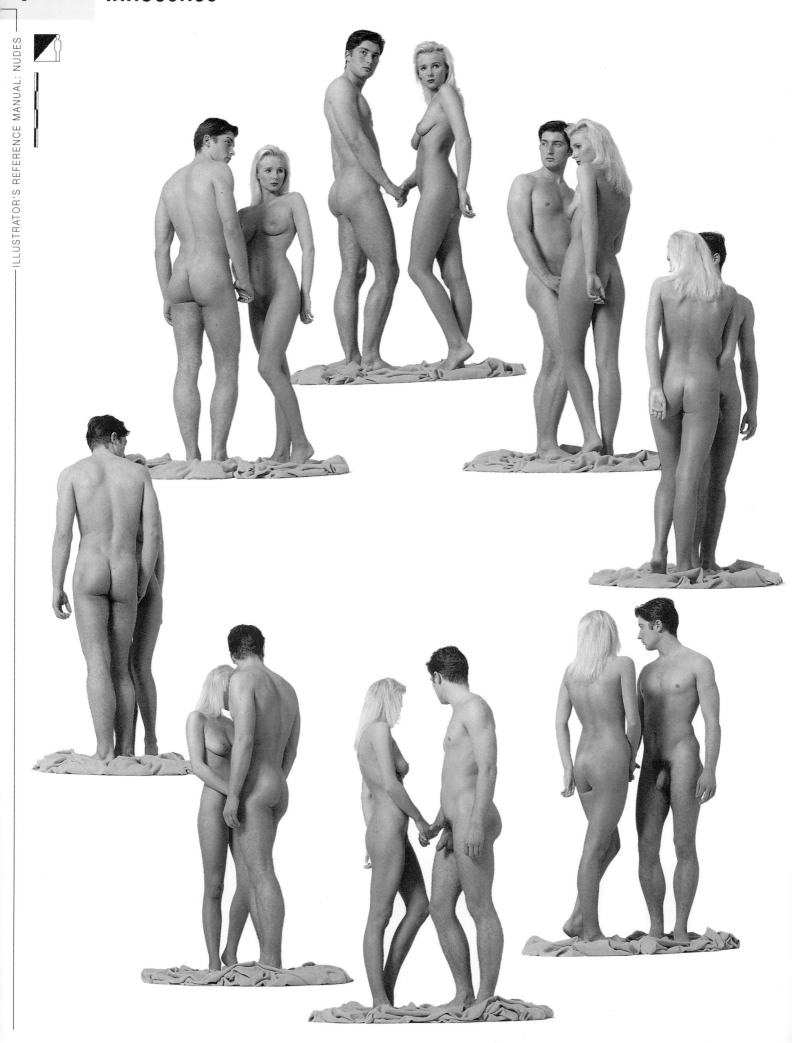

Innocence

7.08

Innocence

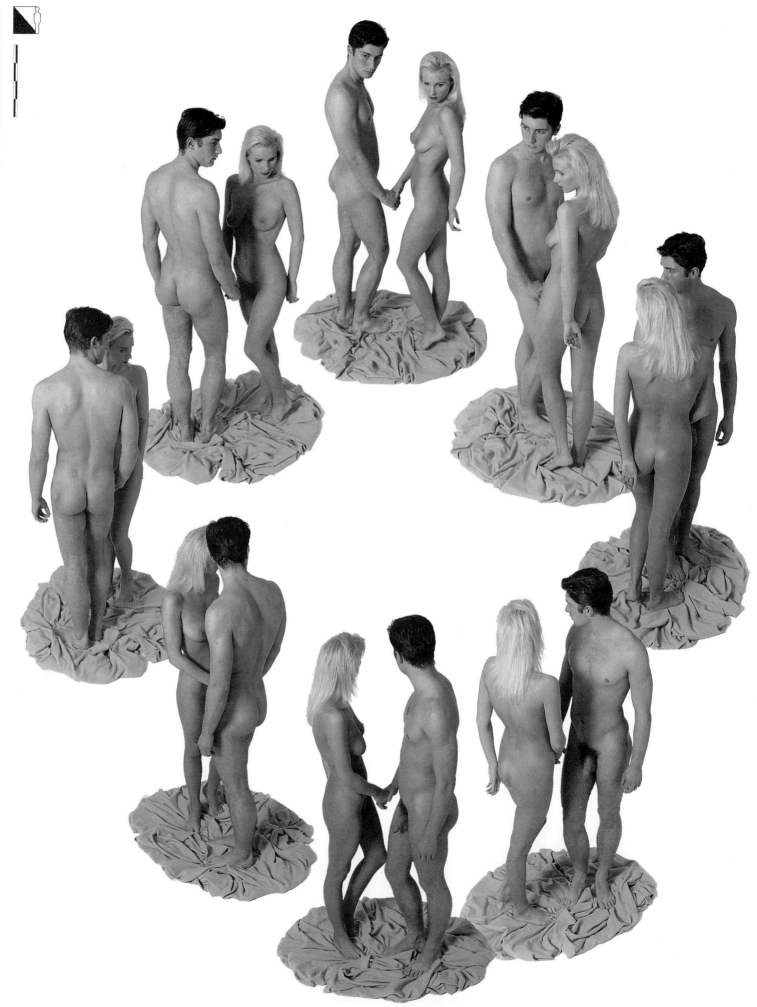

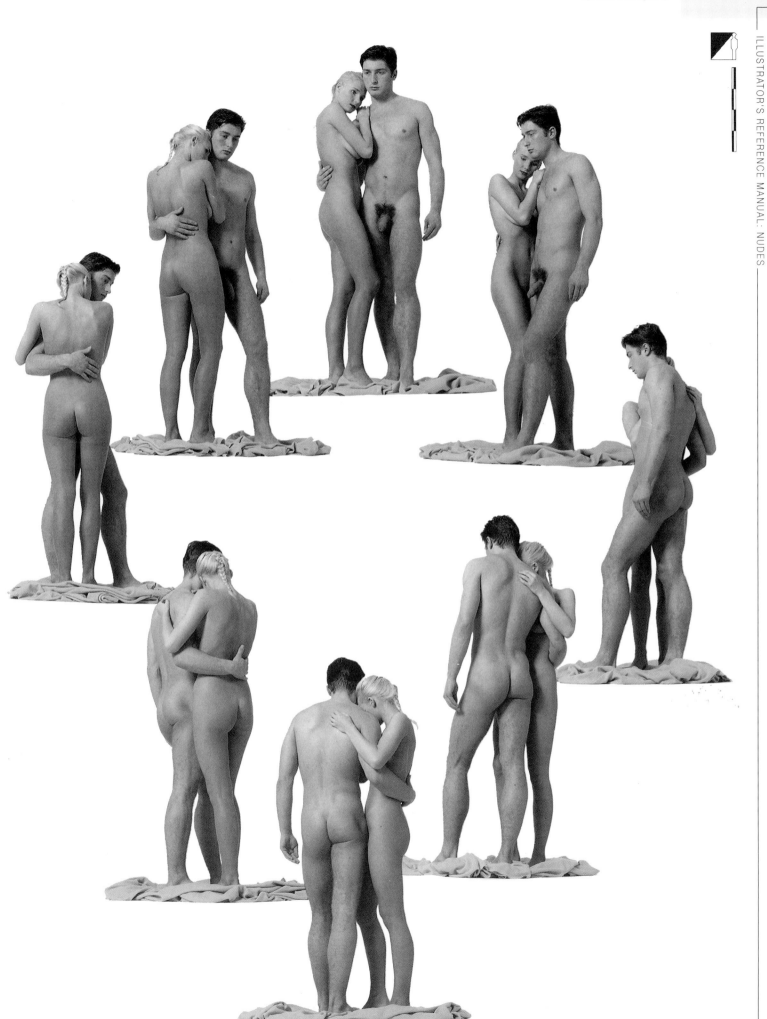

Comest

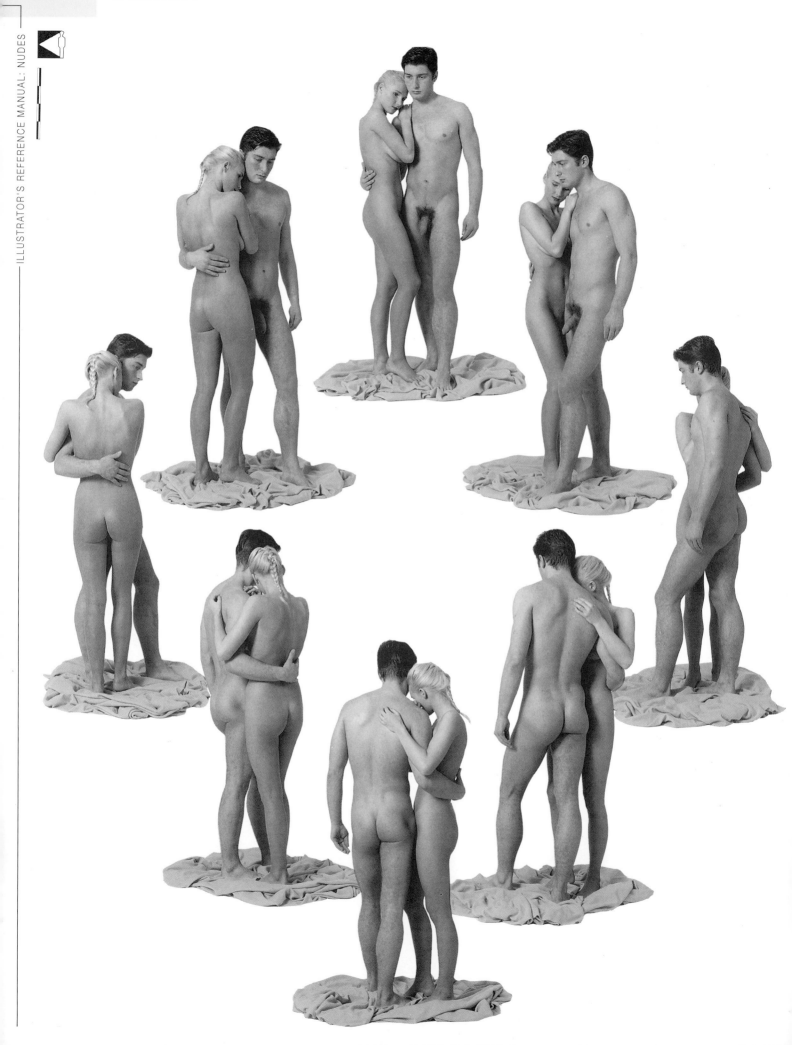

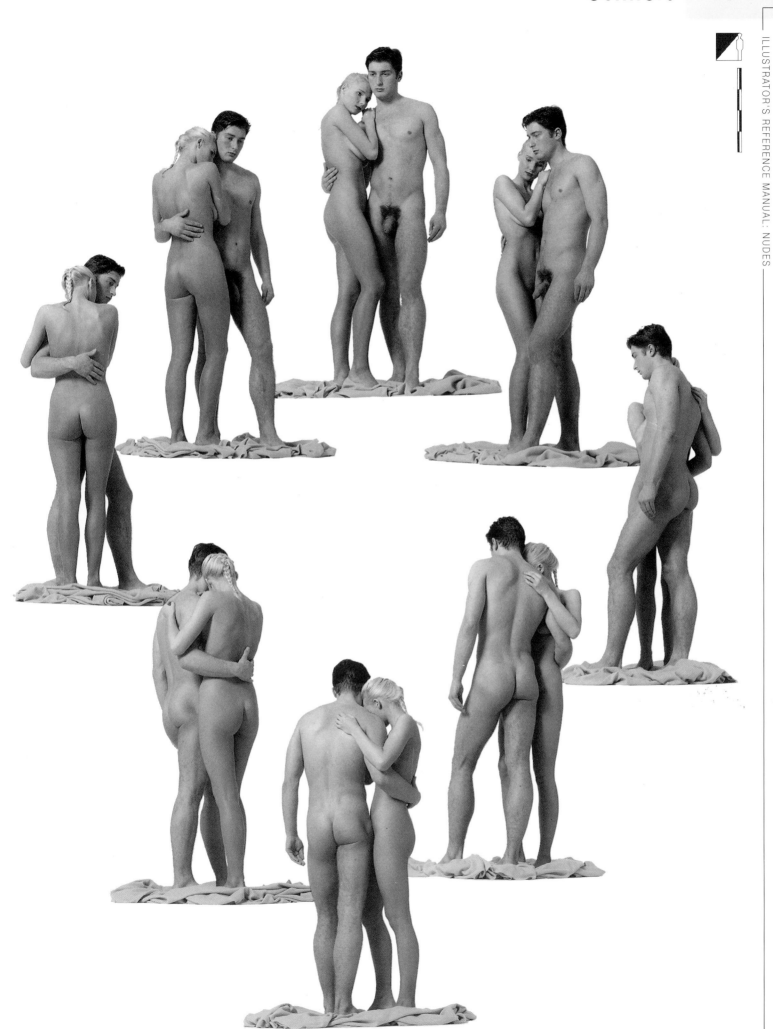

Comfort

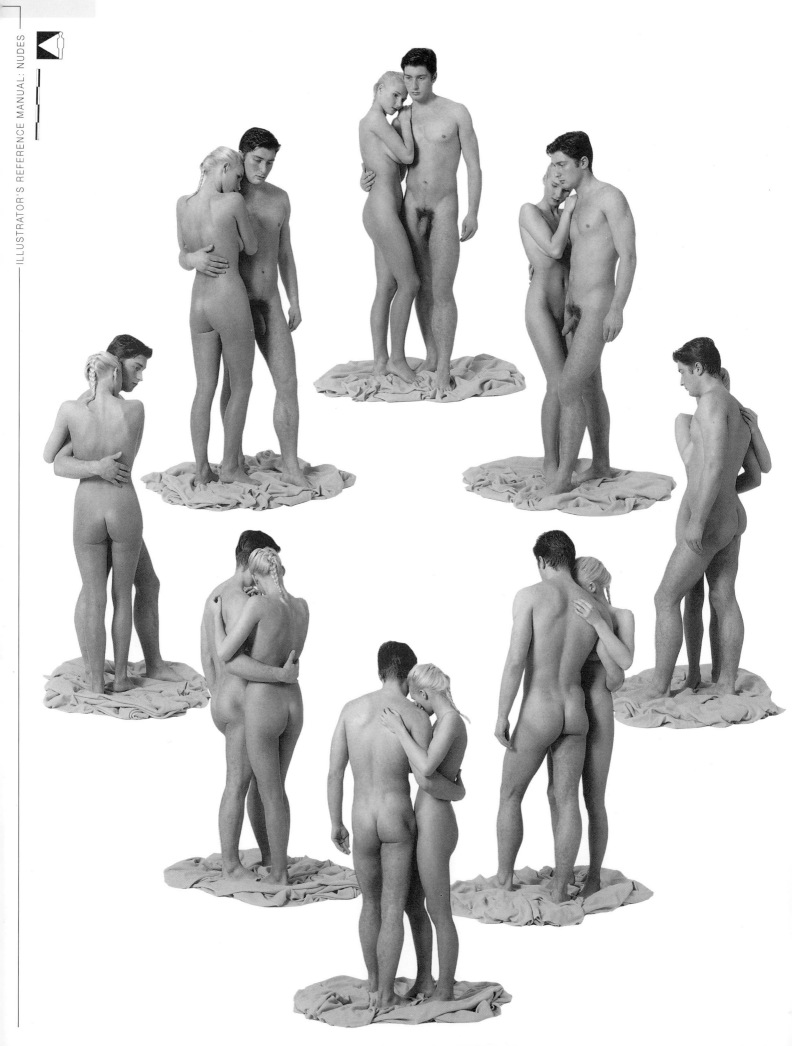

Comfort 7.09

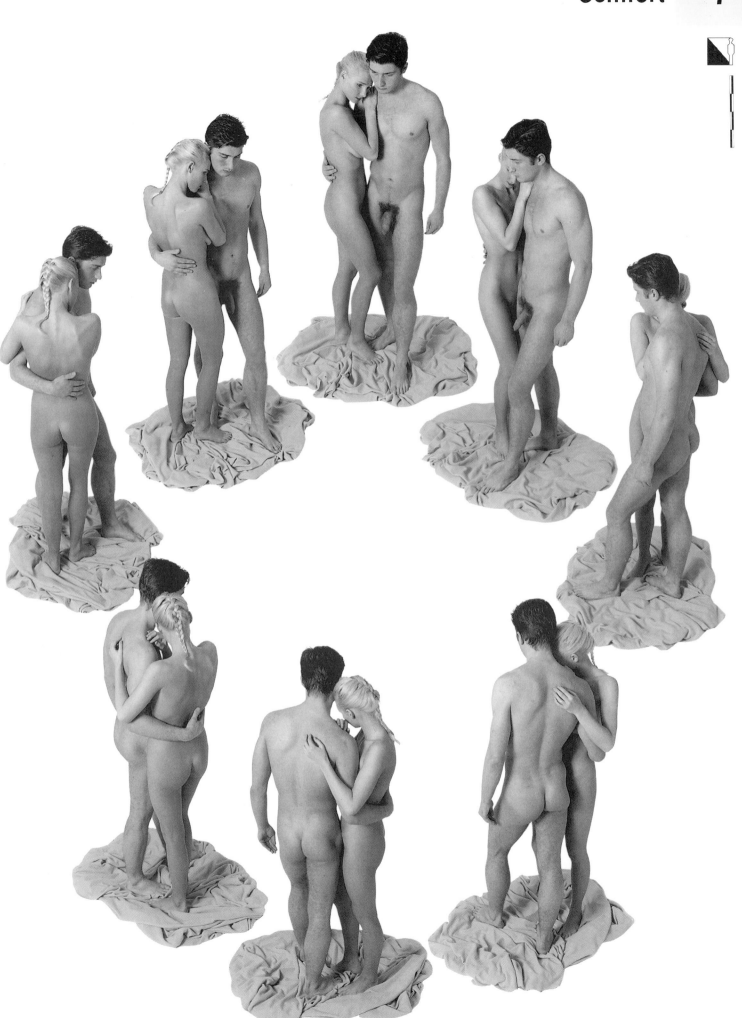

Credits

Quarto Publishing plc would like to thank the models supplied by M.O.T. Model Agency for their highly professional work on this book.